MANAGEMENT OF EDUCATION
IN THE INFORMATION AGE

IFIP – The International Federation for Information Processing

IFIP was founded in 1960 under the auspices of UNESCO, following the First World Computer Congress held in Paris the previous year. An umbrella organization for societies working in information processing, IFIP's aim is two-fold: to support information processing within its member countries and to encourage technology transfer to developing nations. As its mission statement clearly states,

> *IFIP's mission is to be the leading, truly international, apolitical organization which encourages and assists in the development, exploitation and application of information technology for the benefit of all people.*

IFIP is a non-profitmaking organization, run almost solely by 2500 volunteers. It operates through a number of technical committees, which organize events and publications. IFIP's events range from an international congress to local seminars, but the most important are:

- The IFIP World Computer Congress, held every second year;
- Open conferences;
- Working conferences.

The flagship event is the IFIP World Computer Congress, at which both invited and contributed papers are presented. Contributed papers are rigorously refereed and the rejection rate is high.

As with the Congress, participation in the open conferences is open to all and papers may be invited or submitted. Again, submitted papers are stringently refereed.

The working conferences are structured differently. They are usually run by a working group and attendance is small and by invitation only. Their purpose is to create an atmosphere conducive to innovation and development. Refereeing is less rigorous and papers are subjected to extensive group discussion.

Publications arising from IFIP events vary. The papers presented at the IFIP World Computer Congress and at open conferences are published as conference proceedings, while the results of the working conferences are often published as collections of selected and edited papers.

Any national society whose primary activity is in information may apply to become a full member of IFIP, although full membership is restricted to one society per country. Full members are entitled to vote at the annual General Assembly, National societies preferring a less committed involvement may apply for associate or corresponding membership. Associate members enjoy the same benefits as full members, but without voting rights. Corresponding members are not represented in IFIP bodies. Affiliated membership is open to non-national societies, and individual and honorary membership schemes are also offered.

MANAGEMENT OF EDUCATION IN THE INFORMATION AGE

The Role of ICT

IFIP TC3 / WG3.7 Fifth Working Conference on Information Technology in Educational Management (ITEM 2002)
August 18–22, 2002, Helsinki, Finland

Edited by

Ian D. Selwood
The University of Birmingham
United Kingdom

Alex C.W. Fung
Hong Kong Baptist University
China

Christopher D. O'Mahony
The Royal High School, Bath
United Kingdom

KLUWER ACADEMIC PUBLISHERS
BOSTON / DORDRECHT / LONDON

Distributors for North, Central and South America:
Kluwer Academic Publishers
101 Philip Drive
Assinippi Park
Norwell, Massachusetts 02061 USA
Telephone (781) 871-6600
Fax (781) 681-9045
E-Mail <kluwer@wkap.com>

Distributors for all other countries:
Kluwer Academic Publishers Group
Post Office Box 322
3300 AH Dordrecht, THE NETHERLANDS
Telephone 31 78 6576 000
Fax 31 78 6576 254
E-Mail <services@wkap.nl>

 Electronic Services <http://www.wkap.nl>

Library of Congress Cataloging-in-Publication Data

A C.I.P. Catalogue record for this book is available from the Library of Congress.

Management of Education in the Information Age: The Role of ICT
Edited by Ian D. Selwood, Alex C.W. Fung, and Christopher D. O'Mahony
ISBN 1-4020-7430-1

Contents

Editorial

MANAGEMENT OF EDUCATION IN THE INFORMATION AGE

Ian D. Selwood, Alex C.W. Fung and Christopher D. O'Mahony

Since the mid-1980s, computer assisted educational information systems have been developing in various parts of the world and the knowledge surrounding the development and implementation of these systems has been growing. In 1994, the first international working conference on Information Technology in Educational Management (ITEM) was held in Jerusalem. Two years later, a second working conference was held in Hong Kong and following this event, Working Group (WG) 3.7 of the International Federation for Information Processing (IFIP) was established. WG 3.7 focuses on promoting the effective and efficient use of IT in the management of educational institutions. Subsequently conferences have been held in Maine (USA), and Auckland (New Zealand) and Helsinki (Finland). The conferences have engendered a spirit of co-operation amongst people around the world resulting in the publication of five previous books; three special editions of academic journals; numerous academic papers; research funding obtained; and research projects completed. More detailed information about WG 3.7 can be found at - http://ifip-item.hkbu.edu.hk

The content of this book has 5 sections. The first four sections, consists of papers selected from the proceedings of the Fifth IFIP Working Conference of WG 3.7 on Information Technology in Educational Management, held between August 18 – 22, 2002 in Helsinki, Finland. All conference presentations were selected after peer review by an international panel. A further review then identified papers for publication in this book. Thus, the book is not a full conference proceedings, but a selection of papers that were selected for their quality, and capture the range and essence of the conference. The fifth section of the book consists of reports from the discussion groups that met throughout the conference. These reports represent a valuable addition to the subjects covered by the papers and cover key topics of current interest within the ITEM community. They report the deliberations, ideas and key issues that emerged.

1. SECTION 1 - ICT FOR MANAGING STUDENT LEARNING

The two papers in this section examine management issues relating to the use of ICT (Information and Communication Technology) in the classroom.

Leonard Newton's paper argues that problems of integrating ICT into the teaching and learning of other subjects have a managerial dimension that relates to the planning and implementation of lessons. Newton draws on experiences in science education and presents frameworks that offer a means of analysing the beneficial features of ICT in relation to teaching and learning goals and identifying the skills of classroom application required to achieve these.

Chris Thorn's paper examines the problems and challenges that teachers and school managers encounter, in the USA, when attempting to implement data-based decision-making reform efforts, specifically those decisions that influence teaching and learning in the classroom. Thorn argues that while large-scale assessment and accountability data are generally available these are limited to the operational needs of schools and districts for gauging the performance of educational systems. He contends that there are major differences between the evidence used for external accountability systems and the data needed for making instructional decisions on a daily basis in the classroom, and this data is lacking. Thorn further argues that educational organizations have little experience integrating complex data into their decision-making processes.

2. SECTION 2 - ICT FOR MANAGING EDUCATIONAL INSTITUTIONS

This section not only demonstrates the international nature of the conference, and this publication, with papers reporting on ITEM in Australia, Botswana, Canada, England, and Slovenia; but also the scope of ITEM with papers reporting on ITEM in schools, universities and central government.

At the two previous conferences of WG 3.7, the evaluation of the implementation of computerised school information systems (SISs) in Hong Kong and The Netherlands were presented. The paper written by Adrie

Visscher, Phil Wild and Debbi Smith describes an evaluative study of the implementation of the School Information Management System (SIMS) which is used to support management and administration in the majority of English secondary schools. The large-scale survey carried out for this study showed that use of SIMS tends to be clerical, and that the use of SIMS to support school managers is still very limited. A range of problems is identified in the paper and these include the reliability of SIMS, user training (especially managers), user support, and the clarity of the innovation process. However, despite these problems users are in general positive on the effects of SIMS use. The paper concludes that wider and better SIMS use would be promoted by more carefully designed needs-based user training. (Training issues are further discussed in Section 3 of this book.)

Whilst England has a comparatively long history of the use of ITEM, Botswana has only recently started to implement this use of ICT, and the approach is very different. The paper by Coach Kereteletswe and Ian Selwood briefly describing Botswana and its education system before presenting a framework for analysing the implementation of ITEM in developing countries, and subsequently describes the first stages of ITEM implementation in Botswana. Botswana, like many developing countries, has an education system that has a highly centralised management structure, with very few management responsibilities devolved from central government. The approach to implementing ITEM commencing at the Ministry and then rolling out down the system is perhaps unique.

Following a review of the literature concerning the impact of ICT on the work of school principals in various countries, Margaret Haughey reports on her research from Canada, where in the jurisdiction she studied, the process of technology integration is only just beginning. However, she reports that the impact of ICT has already been felt in the principals' offices with principals required to be more knowledgeable about various computer applications, to correspond easily via e-mail, and to organize and retrieve information. Furthermore, she reports that principals are under increased pressure to ensure the quality of their schools, as the district has used the information provided by principals to identify poorly performing schools.

The paper by Arthur Tatnall and Allan Pitman further addresses the issue of accountability of schools. In their paper, they argue that even though the use of ITEM offers many advantages to schools it also serves a role in acting to control schools. The use of ITEM in schools in Victoria, Australia and Ontario, Canada is examined in the paper. The authors then argue that even in areas where management responsibilities are devolved to schools, from central education authorities, ITEM may actually play a significant role in tightening the coupling between schools and central education authorities.

This they argue leads to greater standardisation and control over the way that schools perform their administrative functions.

Much of the previously published literature on ITEM has concentrated on the use of information systems in schools. The final two papers in this section, however, discuss the use of ITEM at University level. Nonetheless, a pertinent issue raised when examining ITEM use in higher education may well have a parallel in schools and vice versa. Chris Thorn's paper (see Section 1) raised the issue of access to appropriate student records, by teaching staff, so that data could be used for planning teaching and learning. The papers by Bill Davey and Arthur Tatnall, and Marko Bajec, Viljan Mahnič and Marjan Krisper both deal with this issue.

Following their concern that student records systems could, in many cases, easily provide much more useful teaching information than they currently do Bill Davey and Arthur Tatnall's paper reports on research into student records systems. The paper argues that academics, in their teaching role, should be regarded as significant stakeholders in student records systems, but notes that often their needs have not been considered. Research was initially undertaken in three universities in Australia but was followed by a larger international survey. The question of how well university administrative systems meet the needs of teaching, and what information university teachers might wish to obtain from such systems, but cannot obtain now, is also discussed. To determine the focus of a university student records system, and how well it relates to classroom teaching needs, a *'litmus test'* was developed and trialled.

Marko Bajec, Viljan Mahnič and Marjan Krisper's paper describes how as part of the University of Ljubljana's Information Systems (IS) Strategy Plan their current student records IS was renovated using a technology which seemed to be very promising in developing integrated, user-centric IT solutions. The strategy plan had revealed many weaknesses and disadvantages with the university IS. One of these was the lack of the possibility to utilize e-business technology. The paper briefly describes the University of Ljubljana's IS Strategy Plan and discusses some characteristics of the portal technology that enabled wider, user-centric access of the student records IS.

3.   SECTION 3 - THE MANAGEMENT OF E-LEARNING

In this section, the focus is once again, predominantly on the University sector. The four papers published here examine various aspects of the management of e-learning. Alex Fung and Jenilyn Ledesma describe how, at the Hong Kong Baptist University (HKBU), a Taskforce was set up to promote web based teaching and learning activities within the university community. Their paper reports some preliminary findings on the nature, approach and progress made by the Taskforce during its first phase of implementation of the WebCT – the current platform for the initiative. The paper sheds light on what academic staff at HKBU need to support their use of web based technologies for teaching and learning and highlights that the potential benefit of IT can be realized provided careful attention is paid to a range of factors.

The remaining two papers in this section deal with the development of e-learning systems, and a central concern to all the authors is collaboration – and how e-learning systems may address this concern. Based on a concern that Learning Management Systems (LMS) suffer from lack of flexibility in sharing and exchanging learning resources and learner data, Rima Abdallah, Abdelmalek Benzekri, Ali El Hajj and Ibrahim Moukarzel present in their paper a new Web Based Training/Education (WBT/E) Model based on the Learning Technology Systems Architecture (LTSA) standard and on the WBT Model of the Enhance Project. To illustrate the model, a scenario of collaborative learning is presented. WebCT was used as the distance-learning platform, RealNetworks family for manipulating synchronized multimedia courses integrated in WebCT, and Microsoft NetMeeting for providing audio/video/sharing of application among the collaborators.

In the paper by Mario Marrero, Celso Perdomo, Jorge Rodríguez and Antonio González, the authors argue that in the past the focus of much research concerned with the implementation of information technologies in organizations, was on the interaction between a human and a machine. However, they feel that this approach ignores the fact that many tasks in organizations necessarily have a collaborative aspect. In their paper Marrero et al. discuss groupware technologies and introduce an Internet-based tool, HTC, which is a collaborative and distributed application where an individual workspace can be created for each user, which can in turn, be shared partially or totally with other HTC users. The paper then describes the integration process of HTC in the University of Las Palmas de Gran Canaria and its use by students and academics.

4. SECTION 4 – ICT TRAINING FOR EDUCATIONAL PROFESSIONALS

Training to educationalists to use ICT effectively for administration management and, teaching and learning, has been a recurrent issue at previous ITEM and other conferences concerned with ICT in education. The following three papers again address this issue. The need for ongoing training is demonstrated in Christopher O'Mahony's paper. The papers presented by Javier Osorio and Maureen Lambert and Patrick Nolan both present models for the effective implementation of training programmes

Christopher O'Mahony's paper reports on a survey that investigated the use of ICT by academic and non-academic staff at an independent English secondary school. Three key areas were investigated: access to ICT inside and outside the school, the perceived and desired ICT ability of staff, and issues preventing increased use of ICT in teaching, learning and administration. The paper concludes that despite recognition that there is a growing obligation and desire to incorporate ICT elements into teaching and learning, including lesson preparation, teachers still report concerns with training and the amount of time available to improve their skills with ICT, and that there is a need for a well-defined programme for professional development.

Maureen Lambert and Patrick Nolan's paper asserts that ICT implementation in educational institutions has proved to be problematic with outcomes falling far below expectations. They suggest that a solution is a more holistic approach to professional development that takes into account the school-learning environment, including school culture, in an effort to develop educational practitioners as 'all-round' capable ICT-using professionals. They argue that professional development should be linked directly to the contexts where ICT may be used professionally and that development will be most effective by identifying and addressing two simultaneous pathways namely, learning and teaching, and administration and management. To this end, the paper proposes, develops and explains a model of professional development in ICT for teachers.

The objective of the paper by Javier Osorio is to develop a framework for evaluating the likelihood of success in the development of training courses for ITEM systems at managerial level. The paper argues that environmental factors can influence greatly the success of any training course. A review of the literature on contextual factors affecting the training process where variables such as ICT, management, organisational features and managers' profile are present, was undertaken from this review, a list of factors arose. The paper then puts forward and examines a systematic method to analyse the influence of such factors on the global attractiveness of the training process' environment.

5. SECTION 5 – REPORTS FROM DISCUSSION GROUPS

The three papers in this Section of the book are reports from the three discussion groups that met at various times throughout the conference. The reports cover three key topics of current interest within the ITEM community - The Management of e-Learning, Management Systems in the Classroom and Core Competences for ITEM.

The discussion group on the Management of e-Learning was chaired by Alex Fung and explored and addressed several areas regarding the management of e-Learning. Building on the discussion, six issues were identified by the end of the conference. These 6 issues - Definition of e-Learning; Visions of e-Learning [Dreams for the new education system]; How to get there with the support of technology; Changes needed to support e-Learning; Different roles to make e-Learning operational; and other issues and points to ponder provide the structure for this discussion paper.

The discussion group chaired by Adrie Visscher and Leonard Newton considered Management Systems in the Classroom prospects for the future. The paper examines some issues related to the use of Management Information Systems (MIS) in classroom contexts and considers some possible future needs of teachers that may present challenges to the designers of the next generation of MIS tools. The key issue that group felt needed addressing - is how MIS users might more effectively exploit their potential in individual classrooms: particularly in ways that support both the broad standards agenda and, more importantly, the achievements of individual learners.

The third discussion group chaired by Ian Selwood had the mandate to explore the Core Competences required for ITEM. The concern here arose from the fact that it was perceived that attempts to introduce new technologies into educational institutions often lacked coherent and effective training programmes. Having reviewed what literature exists on this topic the discussion group developed a competency based model or framework, which should enable educational institutions to plan their ITEM training and achieve an ITEM-competent staff. The report from the discussion group therefore reviews the literature, presents what the group considers to be a unique and important model, and discusses the advantages of the approach suggested in the model, prior to making the point that further work is needed to elaborate the model.

SECTION 1

ICT FOR MANAGING STUDENT LEARNING

1

MANAGEMENT AND THE USE OF ICT IN SUBJECT TEACHING
Integration for Learning

Leonard Newton
School of Education, The University of Nottingham, UK

Abstract: Improving teaching and learning in the classroom is the key issue facing educational leaders in UK secondary schools and information and communication technology (ICT) is being employed in a range of ways to support this endeavour. However, it is in everyday classrooms that the benefits of ICT for teaching and learning are most immediately felt and this is where the leadership vision will be secured. Many teachers feel the pressure to use ICT in their lessons but they are often faced with the problem of where and how it fits within existing teaching frameworks or understanding how it enriches pupils' classroom experiences. This paper argues that problems of ICT integration have a managerial dimension that relates to the planning and implementation of lessons. Drawing on experiences in science education, it presents frameworks that offer a means of analysing the beneficial features of ICT in relation to teaching and learning goals and identifying the skills of classroom application required to achieve these. It is suggested that many of these application skills find relevance in non-ICT activities that may be familiar and that teachers already possess professional skills that have relevance in ICT settings.

Key words: Integration, skills, teaching, learning

1.   INTRODUCTION

Improving teaching and learning in the classroom is the key issue facing educational leaders in UK schools. The use of information and communication technology (ICT) in secondary school education is a focus of widespread interest. Developers of software and users of ICT often extol its virtues and some governments have invested high hopes (and significant financial resources) in the anticipation that new technologies will deliver improvements in education. Yet, the use of ICT in classrooms is problematic and questions are beginning to be asked about exactly what ICT can deliver for education and how any benefits can be secured. This paper argues that integration of new technology into classroom practice is essentially a problem of management. It draws on experiences from science education in the England to tease out generic issues requiring a management focus for teachers employing ICT in subject teaching.

2.   ICT AND ISSUES OF CHANGE

The use of information and communication technology in education is characterised by change. To take some aspects of the UK experience by way of example, the early appearance of microcomputers in secondary schools in the 1980s allowed teachers to begin to harness the calculating power of these machines to serve teaching purposes. This was especially the case in science education where some teachers had the specialist technical knowledge (and interest) to develop the potential application of new technology in teaching. For example, by linking the computer directly to apparatus for the purposes of making experimental measurements it became possible to collect data for graphical display in software.

Rapid technical developments in the speed, memory and display properties of computer hardware together with concomitant developments in software (much of it tailor-made for the education market) now provide teachers with ICT resources of considerable sophistication and educational potential. However, in England, as elsewhere, developments in ICT have taken place in parallel with rafts of other educational reforms and initiatives and this has sometimes created a climate that has overshadowed teachers' use of ICT. This appears to have been true even where initiatives have been in tune with the educational potential of new technology (Newton and Rogers 2001).

In society as in schools, burgeoning technology has understandably resulted in the technology itself becoming a focus of strong interest. It is perhaps inevitable that the acquisition of the latest technology in schools has trailed that available in the High Street and in many homes. This may have some unforeseen effects in terms of pupils' motivational responses to working in school with older computer technology than they may have in their bedrooms (Keele University / National Council For Educational Technology (NCET) 1997); nevertheless it is a reality in many schools and likely to remain so in the foreseeable future.

The capacity of English schools to accommodate developments in new technology has been constrained by uneven levels of resource and by a lack of ICT confidence in a significant proportion of schoolteachers. The government has sought to address this deficit in skills through pre-service (Department for Education and Employment (DfEE) 1998) and in-service training initiatives (Teacher Training Agency (TTA) 1998). In the context of science teaching, barriers to ICT use have been described in three broad areas: Shortages in computers and related hardware; lack of teacher expertise and inclination (for some) to use computers coupled with a lack of access to machines to address these issues; and finally the lack of clarity of teaching purpose when faced with a wide range of possible options and generic software (Tebbutt 2000). In addition to these factors, Tebbutt raises the need to consider issues pertaining to teachers' workload and pupil characteristics, which might also influence adoption of ICT approaches in favour of non-ICT alternatives. Thus the development and integration of ICT for teaching purposes has proved to be more problematic than technophiles and politicians may have expected or wished. Uneven distribution of ICT resources, deficits in the necessary ICT skills and a lack of pedagogy for teaching subjects with ICT has each contributed to the complexity of integrating new technology into subject teaching.

3. INTEGRATION OF ICT - A MANAGEMENT PERSPECTIVE

The use of ICT in subject teaching involves the integration into lessons of an innovative teaching tool. It is useful therefore to consider how scholarship on the management of educational innovation can illuminate integration of ICT into classroom practice. An authoritative source of such scholarship can be found in the work of Elliot Rogers (Rogers 1995). Rogers suggests that to better understand the implementation of an innovation, attention needs to be paid to the differences between the characteristics of people adopting innovations in addition to the features of the innovation itself. Moreover, scholars of innovation diffusion have seen an individual's perceptions of the attributes of an innovation as useful predictors of the rate of its adoption (Rogers 1995).

With particular reference to educational settings, Michael Fullan has described 'needs identification', 'goal clarity', 'complexity' and 'practicality' as key factors that affect successful implementation of an innovation (Fullan 1991). To develop the discussion further, needs identification raises questions about the relative importance of the innovation and what priority it should be given amongst other initiatives. In England

and Wales, the need to use ICT in teaching is driven by the demands of the National Curriculum. But in science education, as in other disciplines, the attributes of the technology itself and the benefits it brings to teaching might lead teachers to choose to use ICT for its own sake. Goal clarity influences the means by which goals are achieved. Policies and curriculum programs are frequently stated in general terms, but a lack of clarity about specific goals and the precise means of achieving them are major problems in the successful implementation of educational innovations (Fullan 1991: 70). Complexity concerns the degree of difficulty in using the innovation itself, the shifts in beliefs and values associated with using it; and the need to acquire new strategies, resources and understandings to support its use. Quality and practicality concerns the suitability of the innovation for its purpose and that the practical changes which the innovation brings fit well with teachers' situations and requirements. The innovation needs to be practical in the sense that it is achievable. Teachers need to be offered 'how to do it' advice, so that they can learn through first hand experience of the innovation. This will help to enhance professional ownership of the innovation through development of personal meaning and an appreciation of its usefulness (Fullan 1991). An example of the application of these theoretical principles to the use of microcomputer-based laboratories (MBL) in science teaching has been reported elsewhere (Newton 1999).

What emerges from the above discussion is that whatever the policies or requirements, ultimately, successful integration of ICT into teaching is dependent on the attitudes, understanding and actions of individual teachers towards teaching with new technology.

4.   INTEGRATION AND THE NEED TO SHIFT FOCUS FROM TECHNOLOGY TO PEDAGOGY

It has been argued that too strong a focus on technology at the expense of pedagogy has been a barrier to integration of ICT into curricula because of a failure to consider the processes of ICT use (Earle 2001). Indeed the need to focus on the relationships between aspects of computer technology and other classroom events is an issue that has arisen from studies over some years. For example, the ImpacT study identified the importance of understanding aspects of teachers' knowledge in using ICT (Watson 1993). More recently, and at a higher level of technological sophistication, the UK evaluation of so-called Integrated Learning Systems (ILS) suggested that the benefits to pupils of these instructional systems depended at least in part on their use in relation to other, non-computer, activity (Woods 1998). Indeed, when reading reports of research involving classroom use of ICT one is often left with questions of the extent to which any benefits claimed could be directly attributed to new technology, or whether other factors could have a bearing on outcomes. The problem that this issue raises for researchers evaluating ICT in learning environments concerns the effects on outcomes of the context of ICT use and this matter has recently been examined in the literature (Tolmie 2001). Tolmie argues that evaluations of ICT need to acknowledge contexts of use and the interplay between the components of the context, which together constitute the ICT implementation 'event'. This approach is reminiscent of the situated evaluation of software (Squires and McDougall 1996) but, importantly, extends it to include consideration of how mode of use may effect integration of ICT in classrooms.

Consideration of factors such as mode of ICT use, the relationships between ICT and non-ICT classroom activities, the context of ICT use etc. shifts the integration issue towards the management of resources and curriculum. In other words, the managerial functions of teachers employing ICT to achieve particular teaching and learning purposes require closer scrutiny than they have previously received.

5. INTEGRATING ICT INTO SECONDARY SCIENCE TEACHING

A major issue facing teachers is to be able to define what it means to integrate ICT into teaching. What is it that needs to be done in teachers' own working contexts to be able to integrate ICT? In other words, how can the need for ICT integration be operationalised into specific strategies and actions for teachers? The rest of this paper draws on experience of using ICT in science teaching and presents frameworks that are useful to support the management of ICT at the level of the classroom. The argument is grounded in the view that the managerial role of science teachers embraces the functions of preparation and planning of suitable activities using ICT as well as their execution in the classroom; and that these functions are part of the integration process.

5.1 Lessons from teaching science with ICT

As suggested above it is possible that those wishing to integrate ICT into teaching start in the wrong place; that is thinking first about the technology rather than the needs of the science curriculum. Computers need to be used in the service of teachers and, for individual lessons, this means thinking clearly about the curriculum objectives of the lesson and the knowledge, skills and understanding needed by the pupils. These are the very aspects of the teacher's craft with which they are likely to be most familiar - they are specialists in the teaching of their subject.

Contemporary science teaching has been strongly influenced by constructivist teaching philosophy (Driver et al. 1994) and this puts the learner at the heart of the teaching-learning process. One consequence of this view is that at its best, science teaching should engage pupils in activities in a thinking way. Mental alertness and active participation are key elements of learning in this mode and this is widely accepted to underpin effective science teaching.

At face value, ICT lessons can offer many interactivity and high levels of learner-centred engagement with tasks. Everyday experience tells us that many students like ICT-based lessons but is this just because of the novelty effects (which may fade over time) or because it adds variety and is better than listening to the teacher? The argument presented here is that there are other, more subtle, benefits to science learners that accrue from using ICT to teach science. The introduction of ICT extends the range of contexts in which interactive teaching approaches can be developed and it is therefore necessary to be able to identify the value that the use of ICT can add in these contexts.

5.2   The added value of ICT

A necessary first step in planning any lesson is to have identified specific subject objectives for the learners, integration of ICT then becomes a question of deciding how the use of ICT can help secure these desired outcomes. Achieving this goal requires that teachers appreciate the ways that ICT can add value to pupils' experience. However, this is only possible once the desired lesson outcomes have been identified.

In science education, it has become helpful to think about the added value in two respects, first the intrinsic properties of ICT and second its potential benefits for users. This framework of 'properties and benefits' was first described in the context of MBL activities (Rogers and Wild 1996). For the purpose of the present discussion, the distinction between ICT properties and benefits requires further explanation. The intrinsic properties of ICT tools that can offer advantages such as time saving, the ability to handle large quantities of data, automated operations etc. provide a set of first level benefits. For example, the facility of automating calculation or graphing is both convenient and saves time that can be used by pupils for other purposes. However, whether any time saved can be used for learning benefits is dependent on the mode of use of software and this is in the hands of the teacher or pupil, it is not a feature of the software itself. This leads, therefore, to a second set of benefits that can be seen as potential benefits that are not automatic but which derive from the mode of application of the ICT tool in the classroom. Here, it is decisions made by teachers and pupils concerning the mode of use that are critical to securing these additional benefits.

The label 'ICT' embraces a range of software with very different features, for example word processors, graphing software, communications software. It is clearly unhelpful to talk about the range of ICT types as if they were all identical and to suggest that a single model of integration will suit each type is equally unhelpful. The properties and benefits framework has proved to be a valuable aid to thinking about using ICT in science and it has recently been applied to other types of ICT and developed further to consider the types of skills required to exploit the useful aspects of software for teaching purposes (Newton and Rogers 2001). This approach enables the teacher to identify the beneficial features of a software tool in relation to its proposed context and purpose of use.

Understanding of ICT properties and their potential benefits leads to a consideration of skill requirements when teaching with ICT. Skills of an operational kind concern the functional aspects of software use and lead to the first level benefits derived from software properties. More subtly, application of ICT tools to particular science learning purposes requires additional skills and understanding that can provide added value depending on the mode of use and it is here that the contribution of ICT can be developed. It is these so-called application skills (Newton and Rogers 2001) that are proposed to be necessary to enable successful integration of ICT in science teaching and some examples of these skills from science education are presented in Table 1-1.

Table 1-1. Application skills for using ICT in science teaching

VISUAL AIDS e.g. CDROM	GRAPHING TOOLS
• Designing suitable tasks and worksheets, embodying a purpose (teacher skill) • Exploiting interactivity • Viewing with intent; looking for certain features • Reviewing images to seek further meaning • Making comparisons, thinking about links • Avoiding superficial interactivity or 'clickiness'	• Observing the graph qualitatively • Reading values • Describing variables • Relating variables • Predicting • Mathematical modelling

6.   MANAGING INTEGRATION: PLANNING AND ORCHESTRATING LESSONS USING ICT

At this point, it is necessary to review the preceding arguments, which have been concerned to define 'integration' of ICT by identifying strategies and actions requiring management at the level of the classroom.

6.1   Planning lessons

The fundamental issue underpinning integration of ICT is the identification of specific curricular requirements in terms of personal learning outcomes for pupils. These objectives drive the choice of planned teaching approach and selection of learning activities. Planning for teaching means thinking about the needs of learners and teaching for learning involves teachers in understanding the learning process and facilitating pupils in their construction of meaning from information and experience. These are fundamental generic teaching skills and they are equally pertinent in teaching situations involving ICT since they can drive critical the selection of ICT teaching tools.

If an ICT approach is selected, this should be done in the knowledge of the features of the ICT tool itself and the likely value added to the learning experience by its use. This requires teachers to have understanding of the properties of ICT tools and operational skills in their use. Crucially, it also requires teachers to have understanding of the potential benefits that can emerge from using the ICT tool in particular ways in the classroom. This knowledge can be viewed as 'application skill' and it embraces knowledge of what software can do and what it might contribute to the intended purposes. With this understanding, a particular software instrument can be selected because it possesses certain properties and offers particular benefits suited to that learning purpose. As teachers become more experienced in the use of particular pieces of software, so appreciation of the value it can add to learning activities grows. There is a real sense in which increasing familiarity with the use of ICT can foster the development of new activities. Over time, this can lead to insightful new uses for software, which in turn, leads teachers to develop new learning objectives. Rewards of this kind are won through a maturity of experience and reflection on using ICT in teaching

Clearly, novice users will require training in the operational skills required to use software, but once these skills are mastered, then the tool can be employed to serve a learning purpose. For teachers planning lessons to secure specified learning outcomes, task design is informed by knowledge of the potential of ICT, scope of activities, value added by ICT and the skills and experience of the learners.

6.2 Orchestrating lessons - the teacher in action

Teaching is about many things including lesson planning and classroom management. Orchestrating lessons in action is a reflexive process, but at its best, it is underpinned by sound planning. Teachers have many roles in the classroom but in ICT context, the role as provider of knowledge is often reduced since this function is partly assumed by the computer. In contrast, teachers' roles of enabler, challenger, adviser and respondent to pupils can take on much greater importance and it is hard to see how even the most sophisticated software could replace the teachers' skills in interacting with pupils at this level.

Integrating ICT into teaching involves making links between ICT teaching episodes and other related activity. Often pupils' work at the computer alone or in small groups and this apparently 'self-contained' activity may lead teachers to be hesitant about engaging pupils in conversation about their work. However, carefully timed interventions can enable teachers to help pupils working in ICT activities. Interventions help pupils to learn to notice things by focusing attention on what is salient and significant. Reminding pupils about what they already know and can do, and building on this knowledge in new contexts provides a means of linking to other experience, perhaps prompting pupils to make links between observations and their knowledge or experience. These and other teaching roles are of importance in ICT-based lessons and need to be borne in mind by teachers managing classroom activity.

7. CONCLUSION

The challenges of integrating ICT into teaching are real and present a barrier for some teachers. Defining specific lesson needs and goals and engaging pupils in the learning process through activities are key skills for teachers. In the ICT context, these skills must be linked to knowledge of what new technology can offer and understanding of how this is influenced by the mode of classroom application. The managerial functions of planning and orchestrating lessons need to embrace the new opportunities offered by ICT, in this sense ICT can augment teachers' existing skills.

REFERENCES

Department for Education and Employment (DfEE) (1998*). Circular Number 4/98. Teaching: High Status, High Standards. Requirements for Courses of Initial teacher Training.* HMSO, London.

Driver, R., Asoko, H., Leach, J., Mortimer, E. and Scott, P. (1994). Constructing Scientific Knowledge in the Classroom. *Educational Researcher, 23*, pp.5-12.

Earle, R.S. (2001). The Integration of Instructional Technology into Public Education: Promises and Challenges. In *Networking the learner - Seventh IFIP World Conference on Computers in Education.* Andersen J. and Mohr C. (eds) Kluwer Academic Publishers, Dordrecht, The Netherlands.

Fullan, M. (1991). *The New meaning of Educational Change.* Cassell, London.

Keele University / National Council For Educational Technology (NCET) (1997). *IT and Pupil Motivation: A Collaborative Study of Staff and Pupil Attitudes and Experiences.* Keele University, Keele; NCET, Coventry.

Newton, L.R. (1999). *Data-logging in the science classroom: approaches to innovation.* Second International Conference of the European Science Education Research Association (ESERA), IPN, Kiel, Germany, pp.164-166.

Newton, L.R. and Rogers, L.T. (2001). *Teaching Science with ICT.* Continuum, London.

Rogers, E.M. (1995). *Diffusion of Innovations.* The Free Press, New York.

Rogers, L.T. and Wild, P. (1996). Data-logging: effects on practical science. *Journal of Computer Assisted Learning.* 12, 3, pp.130-145.

Squires, D. And McDougall, A. (1996). Software evaluation: a situated approach. *Journal of Computer Assisted Learning,* 12, pp.146-161.

Teacher Training Agency (TTA) (1998). *The Use of ICT in Subject Teaching, Expected Outcomes for teachers in England, Northern Ireland and Wales.* Teachers' Annex A1 TTA, Department Of Education for Northern Ireland, Welsh Office Education Department.

Tebbutt, M. (2000). ICT in science: problems, possibilities and principles? *School Science Review,* 81, 297, pp.57-64.

Tolmie, A. (2001). Examining learning in relation to contexts of use of ICT. *Journal of Computer Assisted Learning.* 17, 3, pp.235-241.

Watson, D.M. (ed.) (1993). *The Impact Report: An evaluation of the impact of Information Technology on children's achievements in primary and secondary schools.* Kings College, London.

Woods, D. (1998). *The UK ILS Evaluations Final Report.* British Educational Communications and Technology Agency (BECTa), Coventry.

2

DATA USE IN THE CLASSROOM
The Challenges of Implementing Data Based Decision-Making
at the School Level

Christopher Thorn
University of Wisconsin-Madison, Wisconsin Center for Education Research, 1025 W. Johnson, St., Madison, WI 53706, USA

Abstract: Systemic efforts to implement database decision-making at the school-level and classroom-level face several challenges. First, most data available within district information systems are limited to operational needs of schools and the district. Second, educational organizations have little experience integrating complex data into their decision-making processes. Third, while large-scale assessment and accountability data are more generally available for gauging the performance of educational systems, there are major differences between the evidence used for external accountability systems and the data needed for making instructional decisions on a daily basis in the classroom.

Key words: Decision support, educational management

1. INTRODUCTION

This paper will examine problems school-level staff encounter when attempting to implement data-based decision-making reform efforts, specifically those decisions that influence teaching and learning in the classroom. Many schools and districts are exploring data-driven decision-making as a solution for improving resource allocation and instructional program decisions. One of the most challenging problems policy makers and educators face in attempting to implement curriculum reforms is that intervention decisions are made at least one organizational level above that of the teachers - the persons actually engaged in instruction.

Any systemic effort to implement a focus on database decision-making at the school-level and classroom-level faces several challenges. First, most data available within district information systems are limited to what has been deemed important for the operational and accountability needs of schools and the district. These data include attendance, discipline, and basic demographic data. District systems will also contain detailed information about human resources, budgets, and other business processes. Typically, the only outcome data available are the results from centrally administered tests (which are often annual events) and grades. While this data is useful to help frame annual analysis of school-level, classroom-level, or student-level outcomes, it is inadequate for making mid-course or interim instructional decisions within a single grade/marking period.

Second, while the issues involved in successful database decision-making are just beginning to be discussed in the literature on educational administration and assessment, an important and growing body of relevant work is emerging from business schools around the world. These studies range from considerations of the role of experts in organizational learning (Albert & Bradley 1997) to multi-dimensional representations of the lifecycle of knowledge (Boisot 1998). Educational journals tend to be focused on application. For example, *School Administrator* recently published an entire edition (April 2001) dedicated to data-driven decisions. This work addresses systemic reform concerns that help to provide both the technical and information resources necessary to support school-level databased decision-making.

Third, while large-scale efforts to make assessment and accountability data more generally available do provide some insight into the performance of an educational system, there are major differences between the evidence used for external accountability systems and the data needed for making instructional decisions on a quarterly, weekly, or daily basis in the classroom. The large gap between the time horizons of state-level testing and the more immediate needs of program administrators and individual teachers in the classroom means that data needs and rules of evidence will be commensurately divergent.

2.   APPROACHES TO UNDERSTANDING DECISION-MAKING AND KNOWLEDGE WORK

There is a growing literature on information seeking, information processing, and information use that provides insights into how individuals and groups identify information needs and then respond (or choose not to respond) to those needs. This work draws on and can be used to frame other work in the areas of group decision-making, knowledge management, and the human factors of decision support systems.

One recent study of information seeking on the web provides an excellent synopsis of what the authors call an integrated model of human information seeking (Choo et al. 2000) summarizes this model. The important aspects of the model for this paper are intersections between the different behavioural areas – the identification of informational needs, seeking to fulfil those needs, and use of information to address the identified needs. The three points outlined in the introduction can be addressed through this model. I will use a school improvement team attempting to create an improvement plan for math instruction as an example case to illuminate several aspects of this information-seeking model. The anecdotes described in this case are taken from lessons learned from working with school improvement teams and from school improvement planning documents.

2.1   Information needs

First, the identification of information needs is a primary problem in any type of school reform or curriculum improvement. As indicated above, much of the data available from district information systems is limited to data useful to make district level decisions. The granularity[1] and temporal resolution[2] of the data available severely restrict its usefulness for different user groups. In the case of an effort to understand current performance and how that performance relates to school and district goals, the School Improvement Planning [SIP] team can examine district accountability reports for aggregate data and school-level and individual-level score sheets from math component of the annual standardized math achievement test and compare the results on these metrics to goals set by the school, district, and/or state for their desired or expected performance.

In this situation, the SIP team attempts to frame a problem in terms of a gap between the observed math performance of the students and outcomes targeted by the accountability goals. At this point, the problem has been

---

[1] Granularity is a term used to describe the level of aggregation of data. For example, attendance data could be listed as follows in increasing finer granularity – days absent this year, days absent this semester, days absent this week, or periods absent this day. The finer the grain size, the more detailed the analysis can be. The tradeoff however, is that the finer the granularity, the more data one must manage.

[2] Temporal resolution refers to the span of time to which a particular datum or data set refer. Annual test scores have the temporal resolution of one year. Weekly spelling test scores have a temporal resolution of one week. The temporal resolution of a particular type of data makes it more or less useful for measuring the state of or the change within a system over a given span of time.

defined as a gap. Typically, the data contained in the accountability system is not sufficient to diagnose the cause of the performance gap. Information on curriculum, teacher ability, classroom resources, attendance, discipline problems, contributing social/home factors, etc. comes from many different sources. The next step is a decision-making process that produces one of two outcomes. Either the SIP team identifies gaps in their knowledge about what might explain the performance gap and initiates a search for additional information or the choice is made to avoid the problem. This avoidance might take the form of a simple denial of the problem – bad tests, high student turnover, etc. – or the team might choose a solution based solely on the easily available aggregate data and make an intervention decision based on incomplete (or nonexistent) data.

2.2 Information seeking

This step is the most intriguing part of the information processing model when examining school level decision-making and the use of decision support tools. Once an information gap is identified, the SIP team is then faced with expressing a model of learning that encompasses the outcome and includes factors that the team feels contribute, either directly or indirectly, to that outcome. It is at this point that they search for new sources of information.[3] This data may reside in teacher grade books, lesson planning software, local databases, locked filing cabinets, etc. The team is faced with the task of assembling data that complies with the model of learning they have expressed. One important dimension of the information seeking activity is differential ease of access. Some data will be readily available in a central data store or in the school office. Other data will be in paper form in or on an individual teacher's desk. Resolving access issues is a constant struggle, since the resource needed to acquire hard-to-find or manage data may exceed its value in the analysis.

Issues of the data's reliability and validity of the data are also important components of the discussion, particularly if students or teachers with substandard performance are to be exposed to serious consequences. In-class assessments, for example, may be entirely valid measures in that they accurately represent the content of the curriculum and related learning standards. The fact that they are scored by different teachers and that the sample sizes are small (individual classrooms) means that scores will not be

---

[3] Some examples include; attendance and tardiness data for individual students, discipline data, results of in-class assessments, seniority and educational level of teachers, quality of the curriculum, quality and availability of professional development in the area in question, etc.

reliable. It is at this point that tools for supporting data collection and data exploration are most important.

2.3 Information use

The information use portion of the model describes the combination of the identified needs, the acquired information, and its translation into action. This is the area where the identification of gaps in student understanding or in teacher professional development are codified based on the gathered information and a plan is implemented to address the shortcoming.

Information use interacts with human tendencies to engage in maintenance of the current practice and accept existing norms of behaviour or to change them. There are many instances where school reform initiatives challenge existing practices, allocation of resources, and the skills of teaching professionals. It is only in gathering appropriate information that newly defined problems can be examined and the results of new efforts can be evaluated. School reform efforts interact with all areas of this model. Policy makers and implementers must recognize these social structures and practices in order to support the desired behaviour and achieve the target outcomes.

3. DECISION-MAKING MODELS

(Choo et al. 2000) provide a second model that parallels the human information-seeking model. This model provides a short hand for a larger decision-making model. The authors argue that sensemaking is the first important activity. This is the process of coordinating beliefs with extant information. The sensemaking process often requires that one engage in knowledge creation – bringing external information together with implicit and explicit knowledge about the current problem. Knowledge creation serves to fill gaps in the sensemaking process – it fills in gaps in understanding. Finally, one then moves on the decision-making process that integrates new understanding with existing rules and procedures that guide action.

Knowledge-based systems allow users to explore many different alternatives in a series of "what if" models. Use of the environment itself can contribute to the user's personal skills as an analyst (Jasinski & Huff 2002). School reform efforts encourage school-level staff to make informed decisions that both operationalize their own long-term strategies for student learning and professional growth as well as align with larger district and societal goals. Decision support systems can help to make sense of the overwhelming complexity of large data collections.

Another important benefit that decision support systems should provide is supporting users as they search for and explore the attributes of alternative strategies. The search for alternatives is one of the most important activities in which a school improvement team engages. Shortcomings of existing outcomes lead to an identification of gaps, failures, and needs.

3.1   Sensemaking

In the case of our example, sensemaking is one of the core activities that is often overlooked in school improvement planning. Planning templates are usually created at the district level as a part of a district's accountability system. Outcome metrics are annual scores or percentiles that apply a single accountability model to all schools. The sensemaking process provides a framework for local decision-making. In this example, when faced by declining math scores a SIP team might look at the subscale scores on that test for both grade cohorts and individual students to see if they observe score declines across the board or in specific areas. This would allow the team to reconcile their local beliefs about the quality of student work and the relationship of existing classroom practices to that work. This process mirrors the information needs process in that is through the identification of what is to be studied that information needs emerge.

3.2   Knowledge creation

The knowledge creation process again can be seen as parallel to information seeking. Knowledge is created through assembling individual understanding, bringing in outside information in the form of possible alternatives, lessons learned, etc. and relating that to information already in use. In the example case, this is likely to take the form of exploring what the math test actually measures. This information is then combined with an understanding of the relevant teaching and learning standards to compare what is measured with what is being taught. This synthesis then frames the gaps in the test and the gaps in the curriculum. This gap analysis combined with the sensemaking process provides a framework for crafting new approaches to the problem.

3.3   Decision-making

Now that necessary new knowledge has been created and the SIP team has a clear understanding of the instructional needs of the students and the areas that the test does not measure, it is time to examine a series of alternatives that would achieve the learning goal. This is another area where teams are likely to find great frustration. Often, schools have few resources for identifying alternative approaches to instructional challenges. They often have to rely on a few professional development days, personal experience, and limited contacts with other professionals outside of the school year. However, the team that takes the sensemaking process seriously – perhaps by neglecting the narrowly focused SIP framework – is often better prepared to make a more concrete statement and choose a plan that fulfils their understanding of the needs in the current situation.

These models are not presented as a panacea for decision-making challenges, but they do provide a more human and responsible framework for understanding the dynamics of successful improvement planning at the school level.

4.   TECHNICAL CAPACITY

There is no single approach to supporting better decision-making at the school level. There are, however, a number of approaches to data collection and analysis that might support the development of more sophisticated questions and a more rigorous search for alternatives. As discussed above, aside from basic demographic data, state- or district-level testing is often the only common assessment metric (aside from grades) that is available for analysis of student outcomes. In the case of elementary schools, in particular, much of this data is kept in paper form in teacher grade books and lesson plans.

Centralized classroom record keeping is possible in some environments. The majority of school classrooms have Internet-connected computers and would, therefore, potentially have access to remote systems for entering classroom data and receiving reports. According to a recent National Center for Education Statistics [NCES] study, the availability of networked computers in classrooms has increased substantially.

Since 1994, when 3 percent of instructional rooms had computers with Internet access, public schools have made consistent progress: in fall 2000, 77 percent of instructional rooms were connected to the Internet, up from 64 percent in 1999. However, in 2000, as in previous years, there were differences in Internet access in instructional rooms by school characteristics. For example, in schools with the highest concentration of students in poverty, a smaller percentage of instructional rooms were connected to the Internet (60 percent) than in schools with lower concentrations of poverty (77 to 82 percent of instructional rooms) (Cattagni & Farris 2001).

While schools and students in urban districts continue be relatively disadvantaged in their access to Internet technologies in the classroom, there have been substantial improvements in technical infrastructure. To cite a regional example, both the Madison and Milwaukee public school systems have made major improvements in network infrastructure and have increased the number of networked computers available for administrative and instructional uses. Unfortunately, the technology alone is not sufficient to support robust data based decision-making.

5.   ORGANIZATIONAL CAPACITY

Technology in the classroom is important, but more important is an expanded vision of what constitutes data. One recent article described Palisades School District, Pennsylvania in which parents, teachers, and administrators conduct two, short, one-on-one interviews with over half of the students in the district (Barnes 2001). This data was collected to provide an additional perspective on how the district was making progress to meet its learning goals.[4] Teachers use the feedback they get from students to reflect on instructional practices, refine teaching approaches, and aid them in selecting curricular materials. An interview team visits a single school and spends the day doing interviews. At the end of the day, the team meets with the principal and the teaching staff to summarize the comments made by the students. The interview notes are left at the school to provide teachers with the opportunity to engage in a more detailed analysis of the responses. The survey was designed to explore and make clear the districts expectations for particular areas of the curriculum in each year. In this way, the administration of the survey both reinforced the districts goals and gathered detailed information about students' progress towards meeting those goals. The fact that the walk-throughs are repeated twice a year and occur each year allows teachers and administrators to observe change more clearly and provides a longitudinal view of student experiences that is often lost as student progress from grade to grade with little interaction between grade cohorts.

---

[4] The 15 minute interviews are based on a structured protocol that is adjusted to be grade appropriate.

The importance of active, focused, local school reform is made even more pressing and relevant by a recent study that shows that the impact of teacher classroom practice is equally important as socio-economic background and ethnicity – based on NAEP 1996 test data (Wenglinsky 2002). Educational improvement planning is happening at the school level and has the potential to have a large positive impact on student learning. One of the things that are missing is an open, reflective, decision-making process that would support school administrators and local teaching staff in their desire to engage in meaningful, locally-led improvement.

6. CONCLUSIONS

There is a long literature on decision-making. The *Handbook of Social Psychology* provides an excellent cross-disciplinary overview and describes structure versus process, riskless versus risky choices, and normative versus descriptive models of choice as the important dimensions of decision-making (Abelson & Levi 1985). These authors suggest several approaches that would improve the quality of decision-making. There are several recommendations that would be particularly relevant for this case (see Abelson & Levi 1985: 274-293).

First, improved access to relevant data – whether the data is locally held or extracted from a district data store – would reduce the school improvement team's uncertainty about the important dimensions of the problem at hand. This clearer view of the gap in expected outcomes would allow the team to craft a more targeted and appropriate response.

Second, providing access to high quality professional development materials in the form of case studies that link practice, materials, and outcomes would help the team expand its search for alternatives outside the narrow box of improving a particular score.

Third, review incentives that reinforce short-term gains over long-term structural improvements. The current climate in many urban schools is one of improve this year or else. Value-added analyses that relate performance to the rate and/or amount of improvement for particular groups of students should be explored as a method for rewarding movement towards a goal and provide incentives for improvement to both high and low performing schools.

Finally, district school improvement planners need to recognize that providing school leaders with highly constrained choices about how to show improvement reduces these leaders' ability to think creatively and limits their ability to search for alternatives that would be most meaningful for their particular conditions.

State and district level administrators need to provide leadership by showing that they value appropriate use of data to support school improvement. They also need to provide professional development opportunities and personal mentoring necessary to make their staff comfortable with the process of needs analysis and program evaluation at the school level. While political accountability and its related metrics are important they are too far removed from instructional practices and provide very little relevant feedback for local, classroom-level improvements.

REFERENCES

Abelson, R.P., & Levi, A. (1985). Decision making and decision theory. In *The Handbook of Social Psychology (3rd ed., Vol. 1)*, Aronson E. & Lindzey G. (Eds.),. Random House, New York

Albert, S., & Bradley, K. (1997). *Managing Knowledge: Experts, Agencies, and Organizations.* Cambridge University Press, Cambridge.

Barnes, F.V.M. (2001). Data analysis by walking around. *The School Administrator*, 58 (April, 4), pp. 20-25.

Boisot, M. (1998). *Knowledge Assets: Securing Competitive Advantage in the Information Economy.* Oxford University Press, Oxford.

Cattagni, A., & Farris, E. (2001). *Internet Access in U.S. Public Schools and Classrooms: 1994-2000* (Print available, PDF File). U.S. Department of Education, National Center for Education Statistics, Washington, D.C.

Choo, C.W., Detlor, B., & Turnbull, D. (2000). *Web Work: Information Seeking and Knowledge Work on the World Wide Web (Vol. 1).* Kluwer Academic Publishers, Boston.

Jasinski, D.W., & Huff, A.S. (Eds.). (2002). *Using a Knowledge-based System to Study Strategic Options.* Sage Publications Ltd, London.

Wenglinsky, H. (2002). How schools matter: The link between teacher classroom practices and student academic performance. *Education Policy Analysis Archive*, 10(12).

SECTION 2

ICT FOR MANAGING EDUCATIONAL INSTITUTIONS

3

THE RESULTS OF IMPLEMENTING SIMS IN ENGLISH SECONDARY SCHOOLS

Adrie Visscher[1], Phil Wild[2] and Debbi Smith[2]
[1] *Faculty of Educational Science & Technology, University of Twente, The Netherlands*
[2] *Department of Education, University of Loughborough, United Kingdom*

Abstract: This paper describes an evaluative study of the implementation of the School Information Management System (SIMS) which is used to support management and administration in the majority of English secondary schools. There has been very little large-scale research on the use of computerised school information systems despite the massive growth since the early 1980s. The large-scale survey carried out for this study shows that SIMS use is particularly clerical and the use of SIMS to support school managers is still very limited. Problems identified include the reliability of SIMS, the degree of user training (especially managers), user support if problems occur, and the clarity of the innovation process. Relevant factors relating to the promotion of SIMS use are identified. Users are in general positive on the effects of SIMS use. It is concluded that wider and better SIMS use would be promoted by more carefully designed user training based on a thorough analysis of the needs of user groups.

Key words: School information system, usability, effectiveness, implementation

1.   INTRODUCTION

At two previous conferences of Working Group 3.7, the evaluation of the implementation of computerised school information systems (SISs) in Hong Kong and The Netherlands were presented. Here, we will present the results of similar research in England. The rationale for these studies was to fill the gap in our knowledge on this important type of computer use in schools, and, by that, to gain insight into the factors that prove to promote successful SIS-implementation.   In England SIMS (School Information Management System) has the largest market share of computerised school administration systems. SIMS is a modular but integrated system in that once entered, data is available between modules.   Briefly, SIMS consists of about twenty modules that support the work of clerical staff and school managers and teachers (for details see Wild & Walker 2001).

2.   RESEARCH QUESTIONS AND RESEARCH FRAMEWORK

The following questions were addressed:
– The extent of, and ways in which SIMS was used in schools;
– The user opinion on the quality of SIMS;
– The nature and effects of the implementation process, and the characteristics of the schools into which SIMS was introduced;
– Factors affecting the degree of SIMS use.

The variables relating to the above issues that were investigated in this study fell into five distinct categories according to Visscher's model (see Figure 1), i.e., features of SIMS use, the implementation process, school organisation, and the intended/unintended effects.   The study assumed possible interrelationships between all these variable groups.   System use was expected to be more intense if users' evaluations of the qualities of the SIMS implementation process and the school organisation are more positive. More intense SIMS use was expected to lead to more intended and/or unintended effects.   For an overview of the variables included in each block, the reader can refer to page 86 in Visscher et al., 2001.

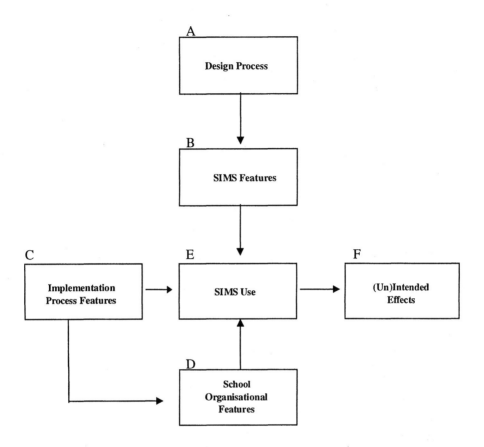

Figure 3-1. The variable groups influencing SIMS use and its effects (Visscher et al. 2001)

3. METHOD AND DATA ANALYSIS

A thousand sets of questionnaires were sent out to a selection of secondary schools in Local Education Authorities (LEAs), in the Midland Counties of England. The LEAs were chosen as they were known to support and promoted the use of SIMS. The schools represented about 25% of secondary schools in England. Each school was sent three questionnaires, which were to be completed separately by the principal, the SIMS system manager and a member of the clerical/administrative staff. The return rate after follow-up activities was 45%.

Data analysis started with descriptive statistics with respect to all variables studied. Furthermore, to investigate to what extent variance in

SIMS use can be explained by other variables in Figure 3-1, those variables that from a contents point of view were considered to be the most promising predictors of system use were entered into regression analyses. The number of available cases required a selection of potential predictors. The 13 selected variables cover aspects of the quality of SIMS (Block B Figure 3-1), features of the implementation process (Block C), and the characteristics of the schools in which SIMS has been implemented (Block D). Respondents' scores were transformed into normalized scores, allowing their mutual comparison, and thereafter entered into recoded pair-wise regression analyses on the use of SIMS by principals, clerks, and SIMS managers respectively. Regression analyses were also carried out on SIMS use at the whole school level (a school use score was defined as the sum of the extent of SIMS use by the principal, clerk, and SIMS manager of that school).

4.   RESULTS

Non-response analysis indicated that the schools in the response group represent the population of SIMS schools quite well with respect to a number of crucial variables like the length and intensity of SIMS use, the nature of the experience of the implementation process, and the impact of SIMS use.

4.1   Degree of use of SIMS

Table 3-1 shows the percentage of staff who used the data directly or indirectly (i.e., used data from the system provided by someone else) estimated within time blocks of time per week. There were some aspects of the results, which were within expectation. For example, clerical staff used SIMS for long periods of time directly for the inputting and updating of data, but a large proportion of them did not use the data indirectly. The results from management staff indicated that they used SIMS for short periods both directly and indirectly. Both the SIMS manager and clerical staff used SIMS directly far more than management staff. Perhaps significant was the very little time that school managers used the system directly, indicating only cursory use of management decision support functions.

Table 3-1. Direct and Indirect use of SIMS

Hours per week	Management		SIMS manager		Clerical	
	Direct use %	Indirect use %	Direct use %	Indirect use %	Direct use %	Indirect use %
<1	36	35	10	43	4	57
1-4	38	46	27	37	7	21
5-10	19	17	21	9	14	13
11-20	6	2	25	4	29	3
21-30	1	1	13	4	25	3
>30	0	1	4	3	21	3
n	205	205	75	75	309	309

Part of the questionnaire was aimed exclusively at principals to obtain some measure of how much SIMS was being used to support management decision-making processes. The principals were asked to indicate whether they used certain modules, which were judged to be able to provide relevant management focussed information. The results are summarised in Table 3-2.

Table 3-2. Use to support Management Decisions in percentages of users (n = 58)

Modules in SIMS	% Use	% Don't use	% Don't know
Analyst	2	78	21
Assessment	38	50	12
Attendance	66	29	5
Cover	41	53	5
Curriculum	24	64	12
Equipment	12	72	16
Exams	66	26	8
Financial management system	78	16	6
Key Stage	19	66	16
Midas	74	19	7
Options	28	62	10
Performance Indicator	16	69	16
Personnel	67	24	8
Report Generator	52	38	10
SENCO	22	62	15
STAR	74	21	5
Timetable	71	24	5
Value added	9	79	12

Some of the modules were, at the time of the survey, recent additions aimed at providing target setting information for school improvement. Two of these, Performance Indicator and Value Added, which would be used for setting improvement targets as required by Central Government, were showing little use. However, there was some indication that some schools used proprietary spreadsheets in preference to the SIMS software modules to make the required returns to LEAs. The overall conclusion is that SIMS is under-utilised considerably as a management tool.

4.2   Perceived quality of SIMS

The second research question concerned the quality of SIMS as perceived by its users. Table 3-3 shows the response to the question "Does the system always work?"

Table 3.33. . Does the system always work?

	Management % (n=205)	SIMS manager % (n=75)	Clerical % (n=309)	Total % (n=589)
No	9	12	10	10
Usually	52	60	74	65
Yes	12	15	13	13
No response	27	13	3	13

The results (only 13% of users experience that SIMS always works!) did not show a resounding confidence in the system overall which in itself could be limiting its greater integration into the administration and management of schools.

Further questions showed that:
- 81% were positive about data accuracy and only 3% are negative;
- 77% were positive about data currency and only 4% are negative;
- 64% were positive about data completeness and only 8% are negative;
- 54% were positive about the ease of retrieving data and 9% negative;
- 51% were positive about the data entry screen format and 7% negative;
- 40% were positive about the data entry system terms with 12% negative;
- 57% were positive about the keyboard entry of data with 8% negative;
- 53% were positive about the predefined printouts with 6% negative;
- 38% were positive about the user-defined printouts with 18% negative.

When asked to compare aspects of the SIMS system with previous systems, such as data accuracy, relevance, currency and completeness around 60% of respondents were positive, with only 5% responding negatively. However, only 62% were positive when comparing the availability of data with previous systems, with 6% negative and 13% neutral.

Results concerning school management showed that 66% were positive about the way SIMS supported management with 27% being neutral and 8% being negative. When asked to compare management support afforded by

SIMS with previous systems 64% were positive, 11% were neutral and 4% negative (21% don't know).

4.3 The process of implementation

Research question three referred to the features of the implementation process by which SIMS had been introduced into UK schools, the organisational features of those schools, and the effects of implementing SIMS. Table 3-4 shows the total number of hours training from both external and internal sources.

Table 3-4. Hours of external and internal training in percentages

External hours	Management (n=160)	SIMS Manager (n=73)	Clerical (n=302)
<1	24	4	5
1-4	19	15	9
5-10	17	18	21
11-20	20	16	18
21-30	6	12	19
>30	15	34	28
Internal hours	Management (n=160)	SIMS Manager (n=71)	Clerical (n=297)
<1	48	73	52
1-4	36	14	27
5-10	11	4	12
11-20	3	6	3
21-30	2	1	2
>30	0	1	4

A large proportion of SIMS managers and clerical staff had undergone some external training in using the SIMS system, many reporting 5-10 hours or more. This represented a considerable expense to schools. However, the results for school managers, with 43% reporting up to four hours external training and 84% reporting up to four hours internal training, together with about forty nil responses for this group, suggests that investment in the use of the system to support management processes was rather low.

Overall, the responses showed that about 20% of respondents were unhappy or even very unhappy with the *quantity of external* training, although for the managers this was 25%. Only 8% reported that they were (very) unhappy with the *quality* of this training but for the managers this was fourteen percent.

Thirty percent of the managers and thirty-eight percent of SIMS managers were (very) unhappy with the *quantity of internal* training although only 9% of managers were unhappy with the *quality* of internal training. However, 27% of SIMS managers were (very) unhappy with the quality of internal training.

An important aspect of implementation was the availability of help for users when things go wrong. Thirty-two percent reported that it was (very) hard to get help from outside school and 27% reported that it was (very) hard to get help from inside school. Overall, 85% of the users tended to solve problems by themselves without recourse to outside or internal support. However, 41% reported that they often used the LEA (SIMS Office) hotline and 39% used colleagues within school to help. The user manual was only used on a regular basis by 21% of staff and the on-screen help by only 17% of staff. According to 60% of users, the overall pace of introduction was regarded about right with 20% reporting on each side of this middle line.

4.4   School organisational features

The majority of staff (59%) felt that the goals of introducing SIMS were clear or very clear with 14% being less than neutral on this issue. However, there was less clarity on the means by which SIMS was introduced to meet the goals with only 44% indicating better than neutral. Ninety-three percent of staff reported that they felt some (or better) encouragement to use SIMS from both the school co-ordinator of the SIMS implementation and the schools' senior management team was needed. At the time of the survey, 74% of the responses indicated a positive motivation towards using SIMS with only 5% being unmotivated. When asked about their feelings if SIMS were to be withdrawn, 86% said that they would be (very) unhappy, with a further 11% being neutral, and only 3% would be happy.

4.5   Effects of SIMS use

The introduction of SIMS into schools had generated several effects in the perception of SIMS users. Table 3-5 presents some of them and it can be seen that higher percentages for all listed effects are found on the positive side. The table shows a rank order of positive effects, starting with 60% of users indicating that the evaluation of school performance had improved due to SIMS, then came the utilisation of school resources (50 %), information for curriculum planning (40%), school internal communication (31%), workload (30%) and finally the positive impact on stress (23%). About a quarter of the respondents thought that using SIMS had increased both their workload and stress.

Table 3-5. School Level Effects of the Use of SIMS in Numbers and Percentages (n=283)

	Negative			Positive		
	Much worse	Worse	% of negative responses	Better	Much better	% of positive responses
Evaluation of school performance	1	4	1	122	47	60
Utilisation of school resources	4	7	3	103	37	50
Information for curriculum planning	1	9	3	73	38	40
Internal communication with colleagues	6	16	8	63	23	31
Workload	15	52	23	63	23	30
Stress	17	48	23	50	15	23

Note: the table does not contain the percentages for the "same" response category. The difference between 100% and the sum of the percentages for the positive and the negative answers concerns the percentage of respondents who neither observed an improvement nor deterioration.

4.6   Factors related to the extent of SIMS use

The fourth research question focused on the factors that had a relationship with the degree of SIMS usage. To investigate the extent to which variance in the degree of SIMS use is explained by (some of) the variables in Figure 3-1, those which the researchers considered to be the most promising predictors of SIMS use were entered into regression analyses on direct and indirect SIMS use at the level of the principal, SIMS administrator, and clerk; and at the whole school level.

Six of the 13 entered variables explained variance in SIMS use indices: motivation for using SIMS at the start of its introduction, computer experience, the amount of external training, and the amount of internal training, users' judgement of the quality of the information that could be retrieved from SIMS, and the length of time using SIMS.

The other seven variables did not explain any further variance additional to the six variables in Table 3-6. These seven variables are: ease of external help in case of problems with SIMS, ease of school internal help, encouragement to use SIMS from the principal, encouragement from the SIMS manager, satisfaction with external training, the clarity of the goals of introducing SIMS into schools, and finally the clarity of the means to accomplish these goals.

Table 3-6. Results of Regression Analysis on SIMS use

Variable	Coefficients	Direct use			Indirect use		
		Clerks	Management	Whole school	Clerks	Management	Whole school
1. Start-motivation	Beta*				4.30		
	Bstand*				0.14		
	Sign.*				0.05		
2. Computer experience	Beta		0.80				
	Bstand		0.20				
	Sign.		0.02				
3. External training	Beta	1.60	1.1	1.40		0.61	
	Bstand	0.22	0.40	0.23		0.21	
	Sign.	0.00	0.00	0.00		0.02	
4. Internal training	Beta					1.70	
	Bstand					0.29	
	Sign.					0.00	
5. Information quality	Beta			0.80			
	Bstand			0.22			
	Sign.			0.00			
6. Length personal use	Beta						0.30
	Bstand						0.15
	Sign.						0.02
	R square	.05	.20	.11	.02	.11	.02

*Beta= unstandardised Beta; Bstand = standardised Beta; signif. = level of significance

The other seven variables did not explain any further variance additional to the six variables in Table 3-6. These seven variables are: ease of external help in case of problems with SIMS, ease of school internal help, encouragement to use SIMS from the principal, encouragement from the SIMS manager, satisfaction with external training, the clarity of the goals of introducing SIMS into schools, and finally the clarity of the means to accomplish these goals.

- Five percent of variance in the degree of direct SIMS use by clerks is explained by variation in external training; for indirect clerical use 'start motivation' explains 2 percent of the variance.
- Twenty percent of the differences in the extent of managers' direct SIMS use are explained by variance in the variables 'computer experience' and 'external training'; indirect managerial SIMS use is explained for eleven percent by variation in internal and external training.
- At whole school level (the sum of SIMS use for all three types of SIMS users in schools) 'external training' and 'quality of SIMS information' as perceived by users explain eleven percent of the variation in direct use; the length system use seems to matter for indirect use (2% explained variance).

Overall, 'external training' proved to be the most powerful explanation of variation in SIMS use as it explains variance in two SIMS use indices. The other five variables in Table 6 account for variation in one of five different SIMS use indices.

5.   CONCLUSION AND DISCUSSION

This evaluation of the introduction of SIMS shows that at the time of this evaluation study, i.e., after about a decade of design and implementation activities, full SIMS implementation had not been accomplished. In other words, even in LEAs where SIMS was promoted, schools do not benefit as much as they could from all the twenty integrated SIMS modules that offer relevant support to school staff.

The descriptive results show that use in general was particularly of the direct, clerical kind. Managerial and indirect use of SIMS are in other words limited. Interestingly and perhaps contrary to expectation, if SIMS was used by managers it was mainly used directly. Quite a few of the SIMS modules proved to be used intensively while others that seem just as important for running schools well were found to be little used (e.g., Attendance, Curriculum planner, Analyst, Alert, Financial Management).

Given the trend of decentralisation towards schools (school-based management) which implies that school policy-making has and will become much more relevant, than when Central Government took most decisions for schools, the search for ways to promote SIS-informed school policy-making is urgently needed. The findings in this study strongly indicate that the extent of SIMS use has relationships with the other blocks in Figure 1. As far as the quality of SIMS (Block B) is concerned there were user criticisms concerning some of the SIMS features. For example, only two-third of the respondents stated that SIMS usually works when they wanted to use it. However, a few respondents were (very) negative about most of the SIMS characteristics investigated. Dissatisfaction with the quality of SIMS possibly is due to the strategy used for the design and development of SIMS (Block A in Figure 3-1; cf. Visscher, Wild & Fung 2001).

Similarly, regarding the process of implementing SIMS (Block C) there is also some room for improvement. User training for about two-third of all respondents were found to be *external* training delivered for about 1-30 hours to clerical staff and SIMS administrators; thus managers had received little training. A considerable number of respondents (about 25%) seemed unhappy about the training they had received.

When experiencing problems with SIMS, user support both internal as well as external to schools is hard to get for about one-third of all respondents. Most users seemed to try to solve the problems by themselves; about 40% of them received support from other sources (the SIMS hotline, colleagues).

As far as the characteristics of the schools in which SIMS was introduced, the goals of the SIMS innovation was clear to 60% of school staff, whereas the means for accomplishing these goals seem less clear (clear only to 44% of respondents). Almost all respondents felt encouraged by their school managers and school internal SIMS managers, and also were quite motivated to use the SIMS package.

With respect to the effects of the introduction of SIMS, the respondents were overall (very) positive regarding all effects studied.

Start motivation, previous computer knowledge, the amount of external and internal training, the perceived quality of the information that SIMS provided, and the length of personal SIMS use explain considerable amounts of variance in one or more of the SIMS use indices. Because these six predictors proved to be critical success factors, they require careful attention in the design of computerised school information systems and in the strategies for implementing them successfully.

The magnitude of external training, especially, proved to be a powerful explanation of differences between respondents in their use of SIMS. The influence of the extent and quality of user training in our view has not been recognized enough, even though these aspects have been prevalent issues in the introduction of IT systems in industry and commerce. In general, the amount of user training should be increased and we need to find out what types of training would produce the best results for the target group. The target group includes adults with considerable work experience at clerical and/or managerial level in schools and the training content should match those features in order to be successful. Careful user training has also much relevance for some of the other predictors of SIMS use (see Table 3-6), as high quality training can fulfil an important role in motivating users for SIS use, by clarifying where and how the SIS can help and add value to their duties. It can also provide the target group with the expertise and skills for SIS use, and show users alternative problem solving strategies they can follow, if SIMS does not do what they want it to do.

Via (quasi-)experimental research designs, alternative strategies for user training must be tested as to their effectiveness. Thus, our knowledge in this area can be refined, the full utilisation of the potential of computerised school information systems increased, and the functioning of schools improved.

REFERENCES

Visscher, A.J., Wild, P. & Fung, A.C.W. (Eds.) (2001). *Information Technology in Educational Management; Synthesis of experience, research and future perspectives on computer-assisted school information systems.* Kluwer Academic Publishers, Dordrecht/Boston/London.

Wild, P. & Walker, J. (2001). The Commercially Developed SIMS from a Humble Beginning. In *Information Technology in Educational Management; Synthesis of experience, research and future perspectives on computer-assisted school information systems,* Visscher, A.J., Wild, P. & Fung, A.C.W. (eds.).. Kluwer, Dordrecht/Boston/London.

4

THE IMPLEMENTATION OF ITEM IN BOTSWANA

Coach Kereteletswe and Ian Selwood
The University of Birmingham, School of Education, Edgbaston, Birmingham, B15 2TT, UK

Abstract: This paper reports on the implementation of a computer-based system for the management of education in Botswana. The computerisation project began in April 1998 and went live, in the Ministry of Education, on the 3rd May 1999. The rollout to the five Regional Education Offices and the twelve Education Centres was ongoing at the time of research (June-September 2001), and the rollout to the 827 state-owned secondary and primary schools was to follow in the next phase. Botswana, like many developing countries, has an education system that has a highly centralised management structure, with very few management responsibilities devolved from central government. The approach to implementing Information Technology in Educational Management (ITEM) commencing at the Ministry and then rolling out down the system is perhaps unique. These factors therefore accorded the opportunity to study the top-down implementation of a computerised information system in a developing country. This paper briefly describes Botswana and its education system before describing research that analyses the first stages of the implementation of ITEM in Botswana.

Key words: Educational management, research, developing country, change management, implementation.

1.   BACKGROUND

Botswana is a large landlocked Southern African country with an area of 582,000 square kilometres (roughly the size of France). However, the population is demographically small, estimated at 1.7 million people, with almost half its population under the age of 15 years. Unlike most African countries, Botswana is culturally homogeneous, and approximately 80% of the population belong to the same ethnic and linguistic group (MoE 1977). Setswana and English are the official languages with the latter being the most widely used in Government, business and education. In 1966, when Botswana became independent, the country was classified by the United Nations as one of the 25 poorest countries in the World (Jones 1977, Taylor 1992). Since independence, Botswana's economy has been growing rapidly in terms of Gross Domestic Product, and per capita incomes rose from US$50 in the 1960s to US$3750 in 1995.

In Botswana, the responsibility for virtually all decision-making concerning staffing, expenditure and curriculum resides with The Ministry of Education (MoE). The MoE has a political head, the Minister of Education, supported by a Permanent Secretary who is assisted by two deputies. The ministry has twelve departments, each headed by a director, and this study focuses on four of these departments - the departments of: Secondary Education (SE), Primary Education (PE), Teacher Training and Development (TTD) and Teaching Service Management (TSM) (see Figure 4-1). TSM, the major focus of the study, is the department responsible for the provision and deployment of teachers to all levels of the education system, in all regions of the country (TSM 2001).

Since independence, Botswana has endeavoured to improve the quality of her education through a number of commissions. The first was 'Education for Kagisano' which led to the adoption of 'The National Policy on Education' (MoE 1977). Initially Botswana opted for 9 years of basic education, but this was later revised to an entitlement for all of 10 years of basic education. This policy led to a rapid expansion of the education system quantitatively; sadly, this was associated with a decline in quality. In 1994, a new education policy 'The Revised National Policy on Education' (RNPE) was adopted (MoE 1994) and this reported that:

> "educational development has been characterised by a massive expansion of school places. For example between 1979 and 1991 enrolments in primary schools rose by 91%, in secondary schools by 342% and at the university by 315%." (MoE 1994: 3).

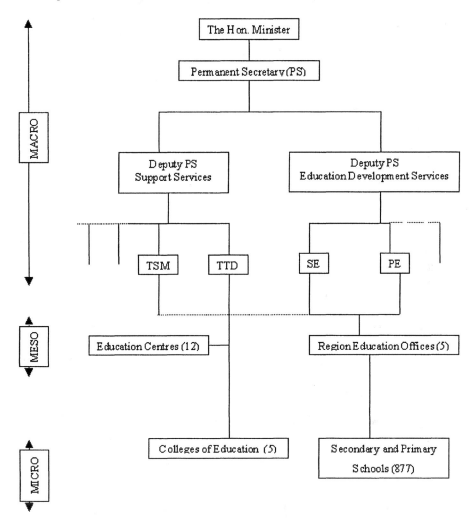

Figure 4-1. Organisation of Education in Botswana (DPSM 1992)

However, research undertaken by the Commission revealed that:

"... academic achievement of standard seven completers is declining. At the Junior Certificate level the pass rate for the Form 2 declined from 85.3% in 1988 to 80.1% in 1991 and for Cambridge (Certificate) from 79.3 to 69.9% in the same period." (MoE 1994: 3).

This massive expansion in schools places demanded a corresponding substantial increase in the teaching workforce. In an effort to improve the management of education, the Government of Botswana conducted a review of the organisation and methods of the MoE (DPSM 1992). The Directorate of Public Service Management (DPSM) that carried out the review and reported that:

> " ....serious organisational problems, including manpower being inexperienced in the overall functioning of the (then) Unified Teaching Service." (DPSM 1992: 3)

Furthermore, the review showed that it was difficult if not impossible to obtain a clear and comprehensive written statement describing the objectives of the MoE at the national level. Additionally, there was no clear statement of the major functions within the MoE. The review recommended some major restructuring in the MoE (DPSM 1992). However, in spite of the restructuring, the MoE indicated in 1994 the need for effective management of the education system, stating that:

> "The increase in the number and spread of educational institutions in the country, especially at primary and secondary levels, presently poses problems of effective administration in view of the centralised nature of the management structure." (MoE 1994: 4).

The RNPE of 1994 further observed that:

> "The success of any education system depends largely on teachers. They are the catalyst of the learning process and on them mainly rests the whole system. They are therefore crucial in the strategy to achieve a more effective and responsive system." (MoE 1994: 4).

Therefore, the effective management of the teaching force was seen as paramount to expanding education and maintaining quality. However, in spite of the reorganisation of the Department of Teaching Service Management (TSM), problems persisted with regard to the service delivery of the department. This was in part due to the manual system in which more than 26,000 teacher records were stored. Additionally, the decline in quality in education had been largely attributed to the lack of resources (i.e., trained teachers, classrooms, science laboratories and equipment).

2.   STATEMENT OF THE PROBLEM

In the TSM, manual processing of large volumes of information was strenuous and time consuming, resulting in inefficiency and poor accountability of managers. Often, it took a very long time for new teachers to get their salary, teachers were sometimes not paid for up to 6 months.

In summary the factors viewed as inhibiting the performance of TSM were:
- Inadequate up-to-date management information
- Lack of visibility of the daily transactions
- Large volumes of paperwork handled daily, which resulted in the misplacement of files and unavailability of data to staff for unacceptable periods.
- Lack of timescales and resources needed to generate management and statistical reports for MoE and/or other interested parties.
- Data available from other systems (e.g. payroll) only provided current staffing information without history or planning capabilities.
- Growing concern over the accuracy and currency of the paper files for teachers within TSM
- There was lack of feedback from other stakeholders involved in the management and administration of teachers (DPSM 1996).

In response to the above problems and the information explosion, TSM was charged with responsibility of spearheading the implementation of a multimillion-pula (£1=P8.86) computerisation project. The project introduced by the MoE was to tailor the "Infinium" software (the package chosen by the government for managing human resources) and to develop an integrated computer network linking the administrative parts of the education system at the macro, meso and micro levels shown in Figure 4-1.

2.1   Research Questions

The study reported in this paper sought to answer the following principal research question: Why and how was ITEM implemented in the department of Teaching Service Management (TSM) in Botswana? This principal research question was broken down into five subsidiary interrelated research questions:
1. What was the purpose of introducing the Infinium system in the department of TSM?
2. What were the stages/phases taken in implementing the Infinium system in the department of TSM?
3. To what extent were the users involved in the adoption and implementation of Infinium in the department of TSM?
4. Was Infinium tailored to meet the needs of the organisation?
5. Were there any modifications in the user systems resulting from the introduction of Infinium?

2.2   Theoretical Framework

The study reported in this paper analyses the implementation of ITEM using a combination of three perspectives as a theoretical framework. They are Fullan's (1991) management of change theories, Fung's (1995) Six-A Process Model and Riggs' (1964) Prismatic Model.

Fullan (1991) viewed change as a four-stage process from initiation, to implementation, continuation and outcome. However, the Six-A model by Fung (1995) provides an elaborated scenario of Fullan. The model comprise a six-stage process from awareness, to attitude formation, adoption, adaptation, action and application hence the six A's.

Riggs (1964) theory of the prismatic society is based on the analogy of white light ray passing through the prism emerging diffracted into the seven colours of the rainbow spectrum. Within the prism, there is a stage where the diffraction starts but remains incomplete. This stage represents both elements of the traditional, fused (white light) type of organisation and elements of the structurally differentiated (diffused light) of 'modern' societies. Riggs was primarily concerned with the analysis of the workings of public institutions of central government and public administration in developing countries. However, Harber and Davies (1997) state that Riggs' theory is a useful explanatory tool for understanding how education departments and schools operate as organisations in developing countries. In essence, the prismatic model is a useful theory in providing the management context in which change is to take place in developing societies.

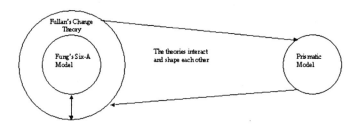

Figure 4-2. F^{2}R Model

Figure 4-2 shows the diagrammatic representation of a bonding of the three theoretical perspectives. The model consists of concentric circles showing the Six-A Process model contained in Fullan's (1991) Theory of Change connected by a bi-directional arrow. The prismatic model is linked to the concentric circles by two-way arrows. These two-way arrows imply that interaction between the perspectives is not a unidirectional process, but rather one in which events at one perspective feedback to alter decisions from the previous model in a phenomenological way. These then proceed to work their way through in an interactive way with a view to emphasising the meaning of the innovation to the concerned parties.

Fullan (1991) comments that the intention of educational innovation is to assist schools and education departments to accomplish their goals more effectively by replacing some structures, programmes and/or practices with better ones. The notion of replacing existing system with better ones is controversial in developing countries. Riggs (1964) observed that in a prismatic society it is difficult to replace the existing (old) systems with the new. Instead, there is a tendency for the new practices to partially displace the old, instead of replacing them. Often, there are problems stemming from the co-existence of the heterogeneous mixture of the old and the new.

Fung (1995) stressed the need for users to participate and be involved in the adoption of innovations for the purposes of ownership and meaningful contribution to the overall design and development of the solution. This is also emphasised in the contemporary literature on ITEM (Fung and Visscher 2001), which asserts that involvement of users avoids ill-conceived designs, and encourages commitment to the new system. Also, the ETHICS approach (Mumford 1983, 1995) is one that recognises the interplay between technology and people, resulting in work systems that are both technically sound and have social characteristics, and this leads to high job satisfaction and creates high quality products.

The F^2R model developed for this research not only considers the change process as seen in developed countries but also the tensions between modern and traditional societies.

3.   METHODOLOGY

According to information provided by the department of TSM, the Infinium System was used by 61 employees in TSM and had been rolled out to three other supervisory departments at the MoE headquarters (SE, PE and TTD). Although the other supervisory departments had Infinium installed, they were not using it and as such could not respond to the questionnaire. The rollout to the five Regional Education Offices (REO) and the twelve Education Centres (ED) was ongoing at the time of research; thus, these were also excluded from this evaluation. Therefore, the questionnaire was administered to the 61 users in TSM.

A total of 58 (95%) users responded to the survey. In addition to the questionnaire, 5 managers, 1 middle manager and 2 technical staff were interviewed. In this paper, the findings will be predominantly based on the analysis of data derived from the interviews, supplemented with some initial findings from the survey. However, as analysis of the questionnaires was not complete at the time of writing this paper, quantitative data will be reported more fully at a later date.

4.   DATA ANALYSIS AND RESULTS

4.1   Purpose for the introduction of Infinium System MoE

The number of teachers employed in Botswana had increased from 1,717 (1965) to approximately (26,000) in 2001. The manual system was proving inadequate in coping with problems of an information explosion of this magnitude. Hence, the prime purpose for introducing Infinium was to manage the personnel records of teachers. The increase in information was however twofold: first, increase in teachers and second, increase in policies generated by TSM to manage the teachers.

Users' perceptions on the need to change were investigated and Table 4-1 shows the results of this. 75% of the respondents firmly agreed with the statement that the need to introduce Infinium HR was *'to improve the record keeping system'* and only 2% disagreed.

Table 4-1. Users' response on the need to introduce the Infinium System

N=58	Firmly Disagree	Uncertain	Firmly Agree
To improve record keeping system	2%	23%	75%
To improve management of information	2%	27%	71%
To improve service delivery in the management of education	4%	33%	63%
To improve decision making process	5%	33%	62%
To improve understanding of management issues	12%	49%	39%

It had also been observed that documents were getting 'lost'. Generally, the accidental loss of documents by error may imply improper filing systems in the department. However, some documents appeared to be lost deliberately and this has other implications. Harber and Davies (1997), Reilly (1987), and Riggs (1964) all note that lack of up-to-date data and ineffective personnel record systems can lead to anti-social acts. Hence, the purpose of introducing the Infinium system was also to end the 'loss' of records. The purpose for the change therefore, has this double-edged meaning in the prismatic society.

The respondents' perceptions on the need to implement the Infinium System seem to point to the need for change relating to three of the four purposes for introducing IT detailed by Cash et al. (1994) i.e. automating, informating and communicating.

4.2   Choosing the System, Managing the Project, and Modifying Infinium

4.2.1   Origination and Policy Implementation

Interviews revealed that there had been three feasibility studies conducted in 1986, 1988 and in 1993 that examined the case for introducing IT into the Government of Botswana. Based on these studies a Statement of User Requirements (SOUR) was developed. A committee consisting of: The Manager of Government Computer Bureau (GCB), Deputy Permanent Secretary (DPS) Ministry of Home Affairs, DPS Ministry of Finance and Development Planning, a Representative from MoE and others, was set up to consider computerisation of the government departments. Thus, decision-making was at the apex of the government's administrative hierarchy. Based on the SOUR the committee selected and purchased an Infinium software license and it became government policy for its departments and agencies, involved in the management of human resource, to adopt Infinium. The MoE charged TSM with the responsibility to implement the strategy in all departments involved in the management and administration of teachers. The TSM department subsequently formed a Project Board (PB) comprising the top managers of the stakeholder departments responsible for the management and administration of teachers. The purpose of the PB was to oversee and review the overall progress of implementation, and decide whether the project should continue after each implementation stage. To manage the day-to-day implementation of the Infinium project, TSM employed an Implementation Manager (IM), supported by an Infinium consultant based in Botswana, and one other person. This group became the Change Facilitator System (CFS).

4.2.2   Involvement and Participation of Users and User Departments

Interview data confirmed that the user departments (stakeholders) were not involved in either the decision to computerise or the decision to adopt the Infinium strategy at TSM. A nineteen-member application team (AT) was set up comprising the Director and assistant director of TSM and approximately three representatives from each division of TSM. The team was formed after the realisation that the SSADM could not supply adequate information with respect to procedures and practice used in the manual system (see 4.2.3 below). The application team participated in defining the user requirements, the new system, and documenting and compiling the procedure manuals.

4.2.3   System Design

Interviews revealed that a Structured System Analysis and Development Methodology (SSADM) was used initially and had included a situation analysis, requirement analysis and definition of requirements, and the design and physical tailoring of the system. Infinium Software comprises of nine modules, however only two of the nine were implemented. These were Infinium Human Resource (HR) and Training (TR) Modules. The initial tailoring of the new system was based on the SSADM and this according to the technical experts did not satisfy the systems tradition cycle. In part, the reason provided for this were inconsistencies between information collected from TSM employees and the actual situation.   There had been no documentation on how the users worked in the manual system and there were differences in the interpretation of their functions.   The technical experts were therefore dependent on 'good guesses', interviewing of users, and data collected from documents that did not reflect the reality on how users worked. This situation reflects Riggs' (1964) view that, in a prismatic society, roles of managers are fused and often not clearly outlined or defined, resulting in formalistic structures that do not reflect the true organisational function.   Consequently, the results obtained from the evaluation of such organisations result in system design failure.

As a result of the SSADM failure, key people in the management of education (at macro level), the AT, were brought in to advise on further customisation of the Infinium Software. There was, therefore, a need to include in the design strategy those users involved in the management of education in TSM. In this way, their involvement may maximise human gains while at the same time achieving organisational and technical excellence. However, it was reported by a member of the CFS that ' *...based on a number of meetings and telling application team members what to do we defined some procedures ...and tailored the core HR system.'* This notion reflects lack of objectivity on the part of the CFS and suggests they pushed their own agenda on the tailoring of the solution, and did not really consult the users.

4.3   Implementation of Infinium System

4.3.1   Awareness, Attitude Formation and User Training and Support

In each category of the questionnaire concerning CFS performance (Table 4-2) the majority of users were 'uncertain' that the CFS did enough in terms of raising awareness, communicating and transmitting knowledge with a small percentage of them firmly disagreeing.   Also, only 19% firmly agreed that the CFS trained them sufficiently with 32% disagreeing. Moreover, it was reported that after training some users could not have hands-on practice because computers were not installed in their offices. However, 81% of the users had prior computer experience before the introduction of Infinium System in April 1998

Table -2. User perception on the performance of CFS

(N=58)	Firmly Disagree	Uncertain	Firmly Agree
The CFS raised my level of computer awareness sufficiently	12%	52%	37%
The CFS transmitted knowledge clearly	11%	48%	41%
The CFS communicated information well	25%	33%	31%
The CFS trained me sufficiently	32%	49%	19%

4.3.2   Procurement of Equipment and Installation

The procurement of much equipment was in October 1998, ahead of the design stage. The equipment was supplied and installed by IBM Botswana. Infinium was installed on an AS400 server that was perceived to have immense stability and the capacity to handle the data.

4.3.3   Government Data Network (GDN)

The GDN was in place at the time Infinium HR was being tailored at TSM. GDN is an electronic communication system for managers only. It therefore, has some serious implications with regard to the rollout of Infinium to schools, as teachers are not considered to be managers. It was reported that due to this constraint an Education Data Network (EDN) was to be developed.

4.3.4   Pilot Project and Rollout to TSM and user Departments (Macro level)

The 19 members of the application team piloted the project. However, as mentioned earlier the 19 members of this team belonged to only the six divisions of TSM. Interviews revealed that the pilot was successful and the project was rolled out to other users in TSM as well as other user departments involved in the administration and management of teachers in the MoE (SE, PE, TTD) and the Department of Planning Research and Statistic (DPRS).

4.3.5   Live running at TSM

It was reported that the system went live on the 3rd May 1999, and it was on time.

4.3.6   Modification of Organisation and Methods

The majority of the informants (95%) agreed that *'there was no significant change in the organisation and methods'*. There were, however minor changes reported on work habits and this was attributed to data capture. It was further suggested that there was instability in tasks and procedures at macro level, stemming from decentralisation of functions to the meso level. It was reported that lack of modification to procedures and conditions of service resulted in incompatibilities in the new ways of working.

4.3.7   Rollout REO and ED and Implementation Constraints

At the time of writing an 80% of rollout to the ED had been achieved. However, there were constraints in rolling out the project to REOs stemming from policy interpretation and implementation, resulting from decentralisation of the functions of the MoE. The other constraints reported were: shortage of telecommunication lines, acute shortage of resources, lack of electricity in some parts of the country, geographical size of the country and lack of skilled computer personnel.

5.   CONCLUSIONS

Botswana is a developing country with a highly centralised system for managing education. Due to the rapid expansion of the education system, the manual system of managing the teaching workforce was not working efficiently or effectively. Initial analysis of data collected concerning the adoption and implementation of ITEM has been presented and shows that:

- Users perceptions with respect to the need for implementing ITEM were mainly concerned with the need to improve record keeping and the management of information. With concerns over 'loss' of records being highlighted.
- The software to be used in the project (Infinium) was chosen by a Governmental Committee, which was concerned with the management of human resources in all areas of government, not just education. Potential user departments in the MoE were not consulted on the decision to computerise or the choice of software. However, Fung (1995) and Mumford (1995) had both noted the need for user involvement at all stages of implementation.
- The Department of Teaching Service Management (TSM) were chosen to lead the implementation of the Infinium System in the MoE and TSM set up a Project Board (PB) to oversee the project and a Change Facilitator System (CFS) to manage the day to day implementation.
- SSADM proved to be inadequate in revealing the complexities of the manual system due to a high degree of formalism in the TSM (resulting from latent functions of managers)(Riggs 1964). This resulted in an application team of stakeholders being set up under the Director of TSM to advise the CFS. However, the attitude of the CFS appears to have been that 'they knew best'.
- Some incompatibilities were reported in the new ways of working. However, users reported that there had been no significant changes in how they worked i.e. they felt that manual procedures had been computerised. This reflects Riggs (1964) assertion that, in a prismatic society, due to the heterogeneous mixture of old and new, the new system does not replace, but instead displaces the old. Fullan's (1991) view that education departments accomplish their goals more effectively by replacing structures and programmes with better ones may not be entirely appropriate for a prismatic society.
- The users were predominately unconvinced with the performance of the CFS, with respect to various aspects such as: keeping users informed, awareness raising, and training supplied.
- Problems in rolling out to EDs and REOs were reported.

Understanding and managing change are dominant themes in management today. The change models proposed and used in developed countries for IT systems (i.e. Fung 1995 and Fullan 1991) may not be entirely appropriate for developing countries/prismatic societies. Therefore, another model, the F^2R process model, was developed drawing on the work of Riggs (1964) and others with experience of developing countries, together with the work of Fung (1995) and Fullan (1991). Even after preliminary analysis of the first stages of this ongoing research project, this model seems to be useful in confronting the complexities of change in transitional societies in a phenomenological way.

REFERENCES

Cash, C.I, Jr., Robert G.E., Nitin, N. and Richard L.N. (1994). *Building the Information-Age Organisation: Structure, Control, and Information Technologies*. R.R. Donnelly & Sons Company, London.

Danzin, A. (1983). The nature of New of Technology, in *New Office Technology: Human and organisational aspects*. H.J. Otway and M. Peltu (eds). Frances Pinter Ltd, London.

DPSM (1996). *Strategy Statement; Computerisation of Personnel Information*. Unpublished

DPSM (1992). *Report on the Organisation Review Ministry of Education*. Botswana Government Printers, Gaborone.

Fullan, M. (with Stiegelbauer) (1991). *The New Meaning of Education Change*. Cassell, London.

Fung, A.C.W. (1995). Managing Change in "ITEM", in *Information Technology in Educational Management*. B. Barta, M. Telem and Y. Gev (Eds.). Chapman & Hall, London.

Fung A.C.W and Visscher, A.J. (2001). Computer-Assisted School Information Systems: The concepts, intended benefits, and stages of development, in *Information Technology in Educational Managemnt; Synthesis of Experience, Research and Future Perspectives of Computer-Assisted School Information Systems* (A.J. Visscher, P. Wild and A.C.W. Fung (eds). Kluwer Academic Publishers, London.

Harber, C and Davies L. (1997). *School Management and Effectiveness in Developing Countries: The Post-Bureaucratic School*. Cassell, London.

Jones, D (1997). *Aid and Development in Southern Africa*, Croom Helm, London.

MoE (1977). *Education For Kagisano, Report of the National Commission on Education*. Government Printer, Gaborone.

MoE (1994). *The Revised National Policy on Education (RNPE)*. Government Printer, Gaborone.

MoE (1999). *Excellence in Education for the New Millennium: A Comprehensive Report on the Implementation of the Revised National Policy on Education*. Government Printer, Gaborone.

Mumford, E. (1983). Successful Systems Design, in, *New Office Technology: Human and organisational aspect*. H.J. Otway and M. Peltu (eds). Frances Pinter Ltd, London.

Mumford, E (1995). *Effective System Design and Requirement Analysis; The ETHICS Approach*. Macmillan Press Ltd, London.

Reilly, W. (1987). Management and training for development: the Hombe thesis, *Public Administration and Development*, **2**, 25-42.

Riggs Fred, W. (1964). *Administration in Developing Countries Countries: The Theory of Prismatic Society*. Houghton Mifflin, Boston.

Taylor, D.C. (1992). *Alternative Models of Secondary Schooling in Botswana, Department of Educational Studies*, (PhD thesis, University of Manchester).

TSM (2001). *Department of Teaching Service Management Strategic Plan*. Unpublished

5

THE IMPACT OF ICT ON THE WORK OF THE SCHOOL PRINCIPAL

Margaret Haughey
University of Alberta, Canada

Abstract: Principals' work has been affected through the use of information and communication technology (ICT): management information systems have regularized, enforced, and revealed inconsistencies that need to be addressed; e-mail has increased and intensified interactions and expectations within the school and with central administration.   ICT have given teachers more information about students but they have also made teaching more transparent and accessible.   Similarly, the principals' work is more visible to central administrators.   As principals and teachers become more comfortable and competent in using ICT it is likely they will develop school-wide instructional as well as administrative responses to ICT.

Key words: Information and communication technology, management information systems, principal's work

Much of the work on information and communication technology (ICT) in schools has focused on the teacher's in-class use of ICT in instruction but ICT have also influenced the work of the principal. Despite this, few studies have examined the impact of information and communications technologies on the work of the school principal. This paper reports on the research available and the findings of one such study. Technology is process and product, figure and ground. It is not neutral, despite our definition of it as a tool, which by implication, we can control. Instead, it is a set of practices that shape us even as we shape them. Its use as a set of management practices shaping administrative work and the work of the school is the focus of this paper.

What do we demand of principals in terms of technology? First, not only has the landscape of principalship increasingly stressed the requirement that principals are key leaders in self-managed schools (Caldwell & Spinks,

1992), but information communications technologies (ICT) have become part of that work. Initially, the pressure on principals was to know the language of computers, from bytes and gigabytes, to RAM and ROM, and in particular, to know what the software and hardware options were in ordering equipment for their schools. Stand-alone computers were followed by local area (LANs) networks. Internet access and privacy issues were to the fore. Teachers in my local jurisdiction were told in September 1999 that their end of term student report cards would be computerized. Principals handled the situation in different ways: one had a consultant come out and demonstrate how to access, fill in, and print individual report cards. Another put a computer in the staff room and told the staff they should all have played one game of solitaire on it by November. The first approach raised the level of anxiety of the teachers; provided with one in-service, they were expected to be able to emulate the consultant. Teachers at the other school, laughed, joked and helped each other as they learned to play, discovering in the process not only to use a computer but also how to calculate percentages, and to complete the report cards.

1.   COMMUNICATIONS TECHNOLOGIES

The introduction of computers into schools might seem to have a greater impact on teachers than administrators but that is not the case. Today's principals are expected to be familiar with computing technologies, to be able to create spreadsheets and to file forms with the central office, to use e-mail and send attachments, to do their own inputting, and often to be comfortable using digital cameras and graphics programs to create suitable memos.

This is not an area of extensive research. In one study, Gurr (2001) interviewed 20 principals in one Australian state about the impact of ICT on their workload. The principals noted the expectations for spreadsheets, e-mail and word-processing, and they also identified various software management systems increasingly used to do budgeting and planning. Such database systems are usually loaded on the jurisdiction's server so that personnel can retrieve information about school statistics or access accounting, budgeting and reporting systems at any time. Most jurisdictions now use management information systems (MIS) to which all schools are connected. This means that data are no longer entered more than once and that sophisticated programming can provide information about individual schools and cross-school comparisons. The system collects more data and provides charts and summary sheets that in turn can influence how the school and its community are viewed. In smaller jurisdictions, principals have less technical support in learning how to operate these systems and such systems are less likely to be tailored to the needs of the district to quite the same degree as in larger districts. Furthermore, principals need to be able to interpret these charts and summaries and understand their relationship to the raw data.

One of the advantages of ICT is its asynchronicity. Principals in Gurr's study talked about the advantage of being able to do school work at home in the evening rather than staying in the building. During the day, principals were often so busy dealing with office visitors, handling student issues, visiting classrooms, and touring halls, that they could not spare long periods of time to do any specialized work. Many principals have told me that they now feel released from the tyranny of the telephone. They no longer have to start phoning and leaving messages for colleagues and central staff immediately they arrive in the morning so that they can receive calls from them midmorning, and hopefully be in the office to receive them. Now they email whenever they can, and can pick up the message when they have a moment. Another side effect of the use of e-mails is that relationships among principals, usually established through informal breakfast meetings, remain important and even intensify since these people are likely to be their most immediate source of information.

Many of the principals whom Gurr interviewed were already comfortable with email and Internet searching. They now did their searching for different ideas online, through targeted searches or through seeking advice from colleagues through professional listservs, whether by jurisdiction, or state or at a national or international level. Once, a principal would have telephoned a colleague about new initiatives or an academic about background research in a particular area--today's principals are going on-line for information. It is not their only source but it is becoming an important one.

Another area where principals are expected to show their competencies in handling communications technologies is in the use of presentation software. It is one obvious way of modelling comfort with technology use (and patience in the face of the inevitable failures) to teachers, students and parents. They are expected to show leadership in helping teachers teach through technology but many were not yet adequately prepared to combine information technologies with good pedagogy (Haughey 2002). Even word processing can radically change not only how principals accomplish work but also how they think and compose text (Gurr 2001). The importance of principals seeing technology as more than "wiring and workstations" was also raised by Valenza (1999), who interviewed several principals and teachers who were using technology effectively. "They saw themselves as learners," she noted. They described their management styles with words such as "thoughtful," "participatory," and "collaborative." All spoke of "we", of the team, of the culture of the school. All recognized the talents of their staff. They continued to look for ways to help teachers teach and to improve the learning environment. They acknowledged the acuteness of the learning curve but believed that it need not be attempted alone. How school cultures are affected is worthy of further research.

2.   MANAGEMENT INFORMATION SYSTEMS

Today's school information systems are increasingly sophisticated. For Bober (2001) such systems provide *"easy access* to *timely* information that has *relevance* and *purpose* with the intention of *empowering* its users" (Italics in original). Such information management systems involve

> "managing a school or district's key functional data including, but not limited to, enrolment, student and staff demographics, course enrolments, class schedules, attendance, disciplinary actions, special programs, grades, standardized assessments, and health information" (p.2).

In a review of school information systems and their effects on school operations and culture, Bober (2001) noted that administrators have moved from student information to tracking changes in the information; from keeping academic information on each student by school to developing and maintaining a profile on the student's academic career; and from using the data to make separate fiscal or academic decisions to using databases that integrate various facets of school life.

Telem (1996, 1999) has completed a series of studies examining the impact of management information systems on the life of schools. In a year-long study (1996) involving observation and in-depth interviewing, he noted that implementation of the MIS brought consistency to addressing decision-making areas, there was more interaction among school staff and autonomy was lessened, teachers were both more competitive and interacted and cooperated more on instructional issues, and the MIS brought a business orientation to school affairs. His 1999 study confirmed these findings and further documented the bi-directional nature of communication and accountability; teachers were held to be more accountable, but they expected to have more information about what was going on. Potential policies and procedures were disseminated more widely and rapidly and issues and concerns were addressed more promptly. He found that firmer student standards were enacted and they were applied more uniformly. Department heads and teachers interacted more frequently but heads were reluctant to give each other unsolicited advice. In a subsequent study, (1997) Telem focused on the new role of the school computer administrator. In large high schools, a site technologist is often hired to deal specifically with the network and its applications. As a result, the person often had a central role in administrative matters, marking unusual data, and checking to see if these were followed up. I am not sure that this would be accurate for all schools but it does alert us to implications of this new role.

It also raises questions about the impact of changing communication and information flows in school systems. Superintendents commonly use e-mail and listservs to share information with schools. Once school-based data are available, central administrators tend to use information based on system level analyses in reports, and are increasingly required to do so as government ministries turn to computerized information flows to monitor the work of school systems. Such information is both more standardized and more available across the system. Its visibility in turn puts pressures on the school to ensure that the data reflect well on the work of the school and the academic achievements of the students. Its availability changes the way decisions are made from single issues to sets of decisions, some managerial and some strategic. There is more emphasis on long-term planning since comparative data can be generated as proxy measures of progress (Bober 2001).

Yeagley (2001) reported on the use of a district management information system in his small "low-wealth" district of approximately 4,500 students. He identified four principles that guided his efforts: instructional change, staff training, communicating results and inviting feedback. He commented that instructional change was his first priority and he wanted to transform data into information that staff could use to improve student learning. While the district had already done analyses of state and national assessments, and looked at individual student results and district averages to identify patterns, it lacked sufficient data for detailed analyses. By integrating data from a variety of sources, the MIS now allowed hidden patterns to emerge.

Regardless of country, much of the initial pressure for MIS has come from the pressures for documented improvement in students' academic scores. Originating in requirements about test scores, districts found that the presence of a compilation of yearly and even semester scores allowed them to use regression analysis and other techniques to identify discrepancies between actual and predicted outcomes. The information also provided teachers with better assessment data since they saw student data across a number of subjects and not just for their own course. The emphasis was on the students' performance and often resulted in more teacher cooperation and team planning to address students' needs. The system also provided teachers with better data for self-monitoring, hence the increased competition referred to earlier. Such systems are not neutral: the information they provide can be used to stereotype students, reduce teachers' autonomy in instructional decisions, and sustain particular agendas such as the use of state-wide or national testing.

Other researchers have examined the implementation of management information systems in schools in Hong Kong, the Netherlands, and in England (Fung & Visscher 2001; Visscher, Wild & Fung 2001). In each case, the researchers identified varied levels of use in the schools. The most commonly used module was for student records.

The extent of use of management information systems is not yet ubiquitous. Most school jurisdictions have some form of computerized data-collection and retrieval but it is often confined to the information required for annual government reports. Many large schools, especially those built in the last decade, have their own school information systems to monitor and assist the information flow. It is likely that many schools have electronic reporting systems, post daily bulletins, and that staff use ICT to organize activities. However, much of this information remains anecdotal.

3.   A LOCAL CASE

To document how ICT has changed the work of administrators, I have begun working with 10 principals and central staff in an urban school jurisdiction. The principals were chosen to reflect a range of contexts and personal interest in ICT integration. Each audio taped interview lasted approximately an hour. I used a combination of content analysis to identify general categories and then close reading to explore these topics in more detail. The description of the study findings was returned to the principals for verification and will form the basis for future annual interviews and more detailed data gathering in the next three years.

This urban jurisdiction employs about 1700 teachers and serves about 32,000 students. It has an integrated technology platform that links all 85 schools; many of those schools have local area networks, and many teachers in these schools have access to a networked computer in their classrooms. However, since the district platform is neither stable nor complete, this jurisdiction can be said to be in the beginning stages of technology integration. The district recognizes the importance of networked technology and has instituted a minimum technology standards requirement for newly appointed principals. This involves about 30 hours of instruction over a four-month period. The focus is on software applications and the major tools and electronic forms have been compiled into an electronic workbook with additional resource sources such as government web sites. The expectation is that these principals will use all the applications in their workbook in obtaining the relevant data required for central office purposes.

The workbook is a management information system and building the workbook has occurred over several years. The goal is to be more consistent and systematic about what is collected in schools, when it is collected, how it is collected, and how it is transmitted to Central Services. The provincial government has increased the types and kinds of information it needs for accountability purposes, and initially these requests were being sent to principals many times a year, often on very short notice and with little turn-around time. Accuracy and consistency were both victims in this paper process. Therefore, the jurisdiction compiled lists of all the different kinds of information required and translated these into a series of forms in the workbook. This will allow compilation of information required by various stakeholders, from the Treasurer and the Superintendent to staff in Learning Services, without further requests to the school administrator. These data, which have to be collected by September 30th each year, drive the amount of funding each school receives and hence principals need to know how to obtain and collate these data. They include student enrolment and achievement data, data required for dollar-driven programs, and budget information.

One impact of the use of ICT is that the district has been able to do a better assessment of students' academic achievement as measured by the provincial tests. Based on the data, the district has been able to compare potential versus actual student outcomes, and identify poorly performing schools. However, at the district level, administrators were not sure of the extent to which principals were using the workbook's data gathering capability to collect information to support their school's goals.

The district uses the email system for most communication. All senior administrators are accessible electronically, which is not necessarily the case concerning telephone and face-to-face meetings. The email system is used to send out agendas and provide current information. The superintendent makes a formal visit to each school once a year. In addition, he meets with all principals once a month. The remainder of his work with his administrators is through e-mail.

In schools that have LANs, most principals have adopted the same procedures with their staff. It is a more efficient way to ensure that staff meeting agendas and weekly or daily bulletins are sent to all staff. Similarly, teachers can use it to correspond with each other about instructional topics as well as administrative matters. Some schools are beginning to receive correspondence from parents via e-mail and others have set up web pages with electronic portfolios which parents can access to view their children's work in the classroom.

The principals all used e-mail for correspondence and had a variety of databases available. Those with an interest in ICT used it for communications with staff such as weekly news bulletins and e-mails and encouraged staff to use it for communication and instructional purposes. They did their own keyboarding and saw ICT as a learning resource. Those who were beginning users tended to focus on the administrative aspects of data-dissemination. For the majority there was a growing recognition of the potential of the medium and some had added or configured databases for their own school matters. They were pleased at their extent of involvement and access to timely information on district matters although their level of knowledge of the MIS databases varied. In some cases, the quality of the school infrastructure had limited staff use. Most schools had web sites and the majority saw these as an information and publicity source only while others used theirs for communication with parents and sharing learning resources with students.

While the district has implemented minimum technology standards, it recognizes that it does not yet have clear plans for implementing them with experienced principals who are not technology literate. They recognize this as a period of evolution, they know where they want to go, and are anxious to ensure that in achieving this goal neither the principals' motivation nor their other goals concerning the role of the principal in instruction suffer.

4.   CONCLUSION

Although this jurisdiction is only beginning a process of technology integration, the impact of ICT has already been felt in the principals' offices. They are required to be more knowledgeable about various computer applications, to correspond easily via e-mail, and to organize and retrieve information. Some are finding that parents use e-mail to correspond with them. Already the district has used the information provided by schools to identify poorly performing schools and so there is increased pressure on them to ensure the quality of their own schools. Some schools have begun to do their own analyses but most are still at the information gathering and communication stages. Visscher & Bloemen (1999) identified training as an important concern. This was true for the principals in this study, many of whom were learning on the job and did not feel they could wait for a district-wide initiative. As LANs become ubiquitous and all teachers have access to computers, then greater transparency, increased interaction, and reduced autonomy will continue to influence and change the work of educators.

REFERENCES

Caldwell, B. & Spinks, J. (1992*). Leading the self-managing school.* Falmer, London.

Bober, M.J. (2001). School information systems and their effects on school operations and culture. *Journal of Research on Technology in Education*, 33(5), Summer. [http://www.iste.org/jrte/33/5/bober.html] 09.05.2002.

Gurr, D. (2001). Principals, technology, and change. *The Technology Source*, September/October.[http://horizon.unc.edu/TS/default.asp?show+article&id=867] 09.05.2002.

Haughey, M. (2002). *Canadian research on ICTs.* Paper presented at the Council of Ministers of Education PCERA Symposium, Information Technology and Learning, Montreal, April 30 - May 1. [http://www.cmec.ca/stats/pcera/RSEvents02/main_en.htm] 09.05.2002.

Telem, M. (1996). MIS implementation in schools: A systems socio-technical framework. *Computers & Education*, 27(2), pp. 85-93.

Telem, M. (1997) The school computer administrator's (new) role impact on instruction administration in a high school: A case study. *Computers & Education*, 28(4), pp. 213-221.

Telem, M. (1999). A case study of the impact of school administration computerization on the department head's role. *Journal of Research on Computing in Education*, 31(4), pp. 385-401.

Valenza, J.K. (1999). The principal who leads on technology is one who learns. *School crossings*. [http://crossings.phillynews.com/archive/k12/principal319.htm] 09.05.2002.

Visscher, A.J. & Bloemen, P.P.M. (1999). Evaluation and use of computer-assisted management systems in Dutch schools. *Journal of Research on Computing in Education*, 32(1), pp.172-188.

Visscher, A.J. & Fung, A.C.W. (2002). *Lessons from implementing computerised school information systems in Hong Kong, the Netherlands and England.* Paper presented at the ITEM 2002 conference, Helsinki, Finland. August 19-22.

Visscher, A.J., Wild, P. & Fung, A. (Eds.) (2001). *Information technology in educational management: Synthesis of experience, research and future perspectives in computer-assisted school information systems.* Kluwer, London..

Yeagley, R. (2001). Data in your hands. *AASA School Administrator.* (web edition). [http://www.aasa.org/publications/sa/2001_04/yeagley.htm] 09.05.2002.

6

INFORMATION TECHNOLOGY AND CONTROL IN EDUCATIONAL MANAGEMENT

Arthur Tatnall[1] and Allan Pitman[2]

[1] *School of Information Systems, Victoria University, Australia*
[2] *Faculty of Education, University of Western Ontario, Canada*

Abstract: The use of information technology in educational management offers many advantages to schools, but in this paper we will argue that it also serves a role in acting to control schools. School systems in Victoria, Australia and Ontario, Canada have in recent years decentralised many of their administrative functions, and similar decentralization appears to have occurred in other countries. At the same time that many countries have been decentralising their educational administration, however, they have often also strengthened central control in other areas, most notably in curriculum and overall accountability. In this paper, the authors examine the use of information technology in educational management (ITEM), and argue that this technology may play a significant role in tightening the coupling between schools and central education authorities. We will argue that this leads to greater standardisation and control over the way that schools perform their administrative functions.

Key words: Educational management, information technology, school systems, control.

1. INFORMATION TECHNOLOGY AND CONTROL

There is considerable evidence that the implementation of Management Information Systems in schools have had many benefits (Visscher et al. 2001) and that the effect on schools has generally been positive. One effect that has not, to our knowledge, been commented on though is that of how these systems affect the control of schools and of teachers performing administrative functions. In this paper, we will argue that School

Management Information Systems (SMIS) have acted to control a number of activities in schools. We hasten to add that we are not suggesting some major Machiavellian plot, or that this control has necessarily been consciously exerted by the people involved in the design or use of these systems. We will, however, argue that it has nevertheless been exerted.

We have observed that, in at least the two different educational systems discussed in this paper, the use of SMIS has led to a greater degree of standardisation of administrative practice in schools. We are not suggesting that this is necessarily a bad thing, and the reason it has occurred is quite simple to find. Whereas in the past, schools in these two systems often followed their own individual directions in determining how to go about performing their administrative functions, they now all use the same software package to assist with this administration. The control arises from the manner in which most SMIS software packages insist that they be used in a specific way. Whereas previously when there were, say, five different ways in which a given administrative tasks could be performed, it is likely that different schools would perform it in different ways. Now the software encourages everyone to perform any given task in the same way. In other words, the software has acted to control the way that this task is performed. Whether this should be seen as a good thing or a bad thing depends on whether you like the idea of standardisation of schools or not, and it is not for us to comment on this. What should be commented on, however, is that this control is being exercised by these systems.

The prevailing rhetoric on educational management around the world has been towards policies of decentralization (Bottery 1999; Chapman 2000), but despite the advantages claimed for it, it is apparent that decentralization is rarely total. Some degree of central control is usually retained in functions such as curriculum and testing (Chapman 2000). We have written more about issues of decentralization and central control in Tatnall and Pitman (2002). This paper will not question the supposed advantages of decentralization, but rather investigate how forms of central control have remained in decentralised systems due to the agency of the technology itself. In particular we will explore the role of information technology in supporting this control. We will argue that the role of IT, through the use of School Management Information Systems (SMIS), is pivotal and investigate how these systems are able to exercise such control.

2. INFORMATION TECHNOLOGY AS AN ACTOR IN EDUCATIONAL MANAGEMENT

An important question to consider when investigating the use of any technological innovation in an organization is the role, if any, that the *technology itself* plays. Various individual humans, including the School Principal, and organizations such as the Education Department and the software developer, are rightly considered as significant actors. But what of the technology itself? How should we consider the influence of the information system?

A research approach often used in investigating the introduction of information systems into organizations is to focus on the technical aspects of the change, and to treat 'the social' as the context in which its development and adoption take place (Tatnall and Gilding 1999), so assuming that the outcomes of technological change are attributable to the 'technological' rather than the 'social' (Grint and Woolgar 1997). Bromley (1997), however, argues that as long as 'technology' is seen as a distinct type of entity which is separate from 'society' the question will always need to be asked 'does technology affect society or not?' The argument that it does leads to the technological determinist position of viewing technology as autonomous and as having some essential attributes that act external to society. The argument that it does not, means that technology must be neutral and that individual humans must decide on their own account how to use it; a view close to the social determinist position. Bromley maintains that neither answer provides a useful interpretation of how technological innovation operates and argues against an either/or stance like this. He argues that we should abandon the idea that technology is separate from society.

Actor-network theory (ANT) provides a useful framework for dealing with the related contributions of both human and non-human actors. By denying that purely social or purely technical relations are possible, and by asserting the world to be full of hybrid entities containing both human and non-human elements (Latour 1986; Latour 1996), ANT offers a socio-technical approach in which neither social nor technical positions are privileged. It deals with the social-technical divide by denying that purely technical or purely social relations are even possible.

The notion of a non-human entity, such as an information system, being able to act in such a way as to apparently exert its own influence on things may seem a little strange (Latour 1988). In ANT, however, an actor can also be considered as a network of interactions, and the network underlying the School Management Information System consists of the information system designers as well as programmers, computers, programming languages, databases, telephone lines and interconnections. In ANT, an actor is any human or non-human entity that is able to make its presence individually felt by other actors, and is made up *only* of its interactions with these other actors (Law 1992). When ANT speaks of the information system acting in some way, this action can always be traced back to an origin in the actions and interactions of the components of its network. Most of the time, however, we can consider the information system as just a single actor. Actor-network theory uses the concept of a *black-box* (Callon 1986; Callon 1987) to describe the process of setting to one side the details of the network that constitute a given actor, and allows a researcher to use this simplification to facilitate explanations. This detail is not lost though, and the researcher can, at any time, lift the lid of the black-box and investigate its contents when this is necessary. We will make use of aspects of ANT to discuss the role of information technology in educational management.

3.   TECHNOLOGY AND SCHOOL MANAGEMENT IN VICTORIA AND ONTARIO

In most countries, primary and secondary school education is regarded as being the responsibility of the State, and is subject to some degree of government control. This control is typically manifested in two distinct areas:
– the system: its structures and personnel, and
– the curriculum: the work content of the schools.

In each of the two systems we refer to in this paper (Victoria, Australia and Ontario, Canada), schooling is the responsibility of the state or provincial government. At the individual school level, both systems have some form of school council consisting of members of the community, teachers and school administration. These organizational similarities, however, mask deep differences in the ways in which power is distributed, as the following discussion makes evident.

3.1   ITEM in Victoria, Australia

The Commonwealth of Australia is a federation of six states and two territories, each of which has almost complete control of its own education system. The only influence coming from the Australian federal government relates to funding for non-government schools, and initiatives with special funding for specific educational projects seen to be of national significance.

In the 1980s, along with most other Australian states, Victoria began to decentralise the administration of its school system. The intention was to devolve much of the administration formerly done centrally to schools, known at the time as 'Schools of the Future', which would then become self-managing. This meant that as well as student administration, assets management and finances, additional personnel tasks such as teacher absences and leave, as well as some payroll and other functions were to be devolved to the school level (Tatnall 1995).

Also during the 1980s, in an apparently contradictory trend, the Education Department in Victoria began to re-centralise the control over school curriculum that it had largely relinquished in the 1970s. At the same time that administrative control was undergoing a process of devolution, the Education Department set up a team to develop and build its own computer-based administrative system. This team was based at the School's Administrative Computing Unit (SACU), which shared premises with the State Computer Education Centre (SCEC). When initial development was complete, SACU began distributing this new system free to all government schools. Birse (1994), who was at that time head of SACU, notes that an important aim of this computerisation project was to improve the financial accountability of schools to the Victorian government, and that in its first implementation it consisted primarily of a standardised school accounting system. Soon the system was extended to cover all elements of school administration and reporting both to parents and back to the Department of Education.

Although the stated purpose of this School Information System was to assist schools in managing their own affairs, they were soon being asked to do most of their reporting back to the Education Department using reports incorporated into this software (Tatnall 1995). It was no secret that these reports constituted an important aspect of the information system, and its designers readily acknowledge that a major aim of its introduction was to make schools more centrally accountable (Birse 1994).

Today, overall control of the system is by the Department of School Education (DSE), a central bureaucracy located in Melbourne, with the assistance of Regional Offices of Education. Each Victorian school is managed by a School Council consisting of the School Principal, elected teachers, parents and community representatives. The School Council or its executive (the School Principal) controls most school administrative functions under the overall direction of the Victorian Department of School Education. Although some administrative functions are co-ordinated at a regional, rather than central level, the only significant controlling body in school management is the DSE. School curriculum remains under the central control of the DSE for years K-10 through its Curriculum Standards

Frameworks (CSF), and through the Victorian Board of Studies (VBOS) for years 11 and 12 in the form of the Victorian Certificate of Education (VCE). The DSE administers a series of standardised tests of all students at several points during their schooling. While schools have some flexibility in interpreting the curriculum, the basic structure and content is determined and standards are set centrally.

School Councils thus manage each individual school with the School Principal (acting as School Council executive) exercising day-to-day control of all administrative functions. Regional education offices oversee some administrative functions and act to assist individual school principals where necessary. The DSE retains overall administrative control, and schools send back regular reports on their finances and other administrative activities. The DSE also retains control over the school curriculum.

3.2   ITEM in Ontario, Canada

Canada is a confederation of ten provinces and three territories, each of which has constitutional control over its own education system. Like Victoria, except at the higher education level, the national government has at best marginal influence on the school systems. In Ontario, schooling is the responsibility of the province and is controlled from the Ministry of Education in Toronto with the aid of District School Boards. The school system in Ontario is one in which, traditionally, a good deal of authority has resided at the local level, at least in respect to employment and supervision of the conduct of teachers. Following the Hall-Dennis Report (Provincial Committee on Aims and Objectives of Education in the Schools of Ontario 1968), curriculum decision-making was also devolved to the local school board level, continuing a trend, which saw weaker and weaker specification of curriculum content from the centre. This period also saw the abolition of the Provincial examination system: individual schools award graduating grades to students in a context in which the content of the final two years of schooling have maintained fairly explicit content requirements in each subject. This took place in conjunction with an apparently countervailing trend of consolidation of local boards (from 5649 in 1945 to 1446 in 1967), a trend that has continued to the point that there are now fewer than one hundred in the province. In the period from 1968, the size of individual board bureaucracies grew, in particular in the support of curriculum developed at that organizational level.

The 1990s has seen a determined effort by government to re-grasp control over the curriculum and organizational structures of the province's school system. Under a leftist NDP administration and later a conservative government, school boards have been stripped of much of their power over finances, teacher working conditions and curriculum. Conversely, School Councils, presently advisory and with very little power, have been established at the individual school level in a first step towards local control over some aspects of the system. Teachers are employed by individual boards, under the rules governing eligibility to teach in the province.

The Province now has a mandated curriculum in place. *The Ontario Curriculum* specifies subjects, their content by grade, and expected levels of achievement by students at each grade level. This is augmented by a series of provincial tests administered by the quasi-independent Education Quality Assessment Office (EQAO) at grades 3, 6 and 9 in literacy and numeracy, soon to be supplemented by tests in other subjects in the intervening years. These tests are specifically constructed to reflect and sample the outcomes specified in *The Ontario Curriculum*. A system for re-certification of teachers on a five-year cycle is being implemented through a newly established Ontario College of Teachers, created by the government through Act of Parliament. The data storage and communication implications of these moves draw attention to the centrality of information systems in the efficacy of their implementation and subsequent operation.

The *BAS* accounting system is used to provide financial data, lists of approved suppliers, school budgets and details of expenditure. Local monies, collected for activities such as school excursions, are handled using *Quicken*. *Trillium* is an information system used in Ontario schools to enable the maintenance of student records, enrolment information, attendance, class lists and facilitating the production of student reports. Individual teachers must complete student reports using the computer-based student report card system, in the standard format determined by the Ministry of Education. In summary, School Boards manage much of the operations of schools, with principals acting as their agents and exercising day-to-day control. School Councils are weak, with principals having primary reporting responsibilities to the Board and, for some aspects, the Ministry directly.

3.3   School e-mail and web use

In Ontario both the School Boards and the various central authorities (Ministry, College of Teachers and EQAO) make considerable use of electronic mail for the transmission of memoranda, advertisements and the like. In Victoria the situation is much the same with notices from the DSE coming to schools by way of e-mail. Ontario Ministry of Education web-sites provide access to policy documents and administrative forms. In Victoria, policy statements and advertisements for teacher appointments vacancies each appear on the DSE web-site.

4.   HOW IT PLAYS ITS ROLE

Most computer software is written in such a way that it forces the user, to a greater or lesser degree, to use it in a certain way. For instance, if the designer of a student records database has decided that 15 characters is sufficient to allow for a student's surname, the names of some students from countries like Thailand will need to be abbreviated. When filling in a paper form, if only fifteen character spaces are left for a surname it is usually possible to write the overflow nearby on the form. In this respect the form acts differently to the computer software.

For most people, the process of writing a paper, a letter, a book or a thesis using a word processor is quite different to that of writing with pencil and paper or, in former times, with a typewriter. That the word processor lets you make corrections without obvious crossings out, that it enables you to insert and move text, and that it allows you to view the document in its final formatted form at any time, make the writing process quite different to working with the other tools. Even different word processors play their roles in different ways. A user of the MS-DOS version of Word Perfect (e.g. Word Perfect 5.1) had to get very familiar with using the computer's function keys, while the user of Microsoft Word was forced to learn to use a mouse. Discussions with a number of former typists suggest that they found using Word Perfect to be no great problem, but had terrible difficulties with using a mouse in Microsoft Word. Other people had the opposite problem.

In the context of school management information systems, we would argue that the software also plays a role that affects the way school administration is undertaken. For instance, if the SMIS requires that certain financial and student data must be collected, but does not require the collection of certain other data, then this is what is likely to happen at the school level. If the designer of the system has not thought to provide an option for recording more than one home phone number and one work phone number for each family, it becomes impossible to enter both parents' numbers if they are living apart, or even if both parents are working. The system has thus acted to control the way that the administrative processes take place. In ANT terms, use of an SMIS, and the resulting additional interactions between all the actors, has resulted in a lengthening of the actor-networks in administration and in curriculum, both within and between schools. These lengthened networks can also be seen in terms of a tightening of the degree of coupling (Weick 1976) that exists within and between schools.

That there has been a tightening of the coupling between schools and the central education authority, at least in Victoria and Ontario, is apparent. For example, in both these education systems teachers must now write their student reports in a standard format using the SMIS, in contrasts to the previous situation where individual schools, and even teachers could, to a large extent, determine the layout and structure of student reports. The use of the SMIS has given head office a greater degree of control in this respect. Within individual schools also, Principals are now able to expect that their teachers will all produce their student reports in a similar format, and in electronic form, representing a tightening of the coupling within a school between teachers and the Principal.

5. CONCLUSION

We contend that an important result of the use of School Information Systems is their tendency to tighten the coupling within schools between teachers and the Principal, and also between schools and central education authorities by coercing schools into performing many of their administrative functions in a standard way determined by the software. We note that Telem (1998) also reports similar findings.

In ANT terms, the software has acted to enforce this way of doing things. While not taking a deterministic position that would suggest some form of causal relationship, we do suggest that use of an SMIS acts to tighten these couplings, so enabling central education authorities to exercise a form of 'control at a distance' over school operations without appearing to intervene directly. King and Sethi (1999) have argued that the use of information technology is fundamental to effective operation of firms operating globally, as it provides a co-ordinating mechanism for their dispersed activities and also enables coalitions to be established. In a similar way we have argued that the use of school information systems provides a co-ordinating mechanism so that central education authorities can keep track of what schools are doing, and also to enable coalitions of human and non-human actors to be established in the administration and managements of schools.

REFERENCES

Birse, J. (1994). Personal communication.

Bottery, M. (1999). Education Under the New Modernizers: An Agenda for Centralisation, Illiberalism and Inequality? *Cambridge Journal of Education* 29(1), 509-528

Bromley, H. (1997). The Social Chicken and the Technological Egg: Educational Computing and the Technology/Society Divide. *Educational Theory* 47(1), 51-63.

Callon, M. (1986). Some Elements of a Sociology of Translation: Domestication of the Scallops and the Fishermen of St Brieuc Bay. In *Power, Action & Belief. A New Sociology of Knowledge? Sociological Review monograph 32.* Law, J. (ed). Routledge & Kegan Paul, London.

Callon, M. (1987). Society in the Making: The Study of Technology as a Tool for Sociological Analysis. In *The Social Construction of Technological Systems.* Bijker, W.E., Hughes, T.P. and Pinch, T.P. Cambridge (eds). The MIT Press, Ma.

Chapman, D.W. (2000). Trends in Educational Administration in Developing Asia. *Educational Administration Quarterly* 36(2), 283-308.

Grint, K. and Woolgar, S. (1997). *The Machine at Work - Technology, Work and Organisation.* Polity Press, Cambridge.

King, W.R. and Sethi, V. (1999). An empirical assessment of the organization of transnational information systems. *Journal of Management Information Systems* 15(4), 7-28.

Latour, B. (1986). The Powers of Association. In *Power, Action and Belief. A new sociology of knowledge? Sociological Review monograph 32.* Law, J. (ed). Routledge & Kegan Paul, London.

Latour, B. (1988). The Prince for Machines as well as for Machinations. In *Technology and Social Process.* Elliott, B. (ed). Edinburgh University Press, Edinburgh.

Latour, B. (1996). *Aramis or the Love of Technology.* Harvard University Press, Cambridge, Ma.

Law, J. (1992). Notes on the Theory of the Actor-Network: Ordering, Strategy and Heterogeneity. *Systems Practice* 5(4): 379-393.

Provincial Committee on Aims and Objectives of Education in the Schools of Ontario (1968). *Living and Learning.* The Newton Publishing Company, Toronto.

Tatnall, A. (1995). Information Technology and the Management of Victorian Schools - Providing Flexibility or Enabling Better Central Control? In *Information Technology in Educational Management* Barta, B.Z., Telem, M. and Gev, Y. (eds). Chapman & Hall / IFIP London.

Tatnall, A. and Gilding, A. (1999). *Actor-Network Theory and Information Systems Research.* 10th Australasian Conference on Information Systems (ACIS), University of Wellington Wellington, Victoria.

Tatnall, A. and Pitman, A. (2002). Issues of Decentralization and Central Control in Educational Management: the Enabling and Shaping Role of Information Technology. In *TelE-Learning: The Challenge of the Third Millennium* Passey, D. and Kendall, M. (eds) Kluwer Academic Publishers / IFIP, Assinippi Park, Ma.

Telem, M. (1998). School Administration Computerization Impact on the Teacher's Role: A Case Study. *Journal of Urban Education* 33(4): 534-555.

Visscher, A.J., Wild, P. and Fung, A.C.W., (Eds). (2001). *Information Technology in Educational Management: Synthesis of Experience, Research and Future Perspectives on Computer-Assisted School Information Systems.* Kluwer Academic Publishers, Dordrecht, The Netherlands.

Weick, K.E. (1976). Educational Organizations as Loosely Coupled Systems. Administrative *Science Quarterly* 21: 1-19.

7

INVOLVING THE ACADEMIC
A Test for Effective University ITEM Systems

Bill Davey[1] and Arthur Tatnall[2]

[1] *School of Information Technology, RMIT University, Melbourne, Australia*
[2] *School of Information Systems, Victoria University, Melbourne, Australia*

Abstract: ITEM systems in the university sector are large. This means they are often purpose-written for an individual university. These systems have significant investment cost when compared with commercial systems. An interesting issue with such systems is the apparent set of perceived stakeholders when measured by functionality of the working system. Initial case studies of three universities in one country showed that existing administrative systems offered little support for teaching purposes. An extended survey over a number of different countries showed few exceptions, and a test was developed to determine if a university ITEM system included the classroom teaching function as a user requirement. The study found few systems catering for even the most trivial of requirements of teaching.

Key words: Information technology, university student records systems, academics, stakeholders

1.   INTRODUCTION

Researchers investigating the use of information technology in educational management (ITEM) often tend to concentrate on the use of information systems in schools. Universities, however, provide an interesting field of study for the ITEM researcher as, opposed to secondary and elementary schools, a university is often large enough to justify a purpose-written administrative system. An individual university needs to store a huge amount of data and is often prepared to spend as much time and money as a sizeable business in designing and producing a system to fulfil its complex administrative needs.

Research at a number of universities has shown that educational administrative systems, and in particular student records systems, often do not provide the simplest of functionality when viewed from the perspective of educational delivery in the classroom. The research reported here implies that the delivery of teaching-related services has been a neglected aspect in the development of administrative systems in universities. In this paper we provide a *Litmus Test* for determining the focus of a university student records system, and how well it relates to classroom teaching needs.

Anecdotal evidence suggests that functions crossing academic boundaries within a university are often completely out of the control of academics who are usually focused within their discipline area. A question that arises for the ITEM researcher in this context is the inclusion of classroom educational specifications within the ITEM systems commonly being produced in universities and whether the picture is cultural, or nationally specific. Our particular concern is with student records systems that could, in many cases, easily provide much more useful teaching information than they currently do.

This paper examines the use of university student records systems, but particularly from the viewpoint of the university classroom. It argues that academics, in their teaching role, should be regarded as significant stakeholders in these systems, but notes that often their needs have not been considered. We question how well university administrative systems meet the needs of teaching, and what information university teachers might wish to obtain from such systems, but cannot obtain now.

2.   IDENTIFYING STAKEHOLDERS, CLIENTS AND USER REQUIREMENTS

The information systems literature points out that effort spent in the determination of stakeholder and user requirements early in a system's development is crucial to its success. The literature particularly stresses the necessity of involving users in the process of designing information systems (Fuller and William 1994; Lindgaard 1994; Lawrence, Shah and Golder 1997) if we want those systems to be used to their full potential. Lawrence et al. (1997) point to a need to consult with users, while Lindgaard (1994) notes that a large body of research has shown that potential users do not make best use of information systems unless they feel that these systems have been designed with their involvement and in their interest.

Both users and clients are stakeholders in the development of any information system, but their needs are not always the same. It is the client who commissions and pays for the development of the system, and the system will be designed to their specifications. A problem arises, however, when the client is not also the only significant user of the system. In information systems development it is not unusual for a system to fail because, although it was technically well written, it did not meet the needs of its users (Meredith and Mantel 1995). Even a well-written system that does not do what all its users want is a waste of resources. As Post (1999) puts it:

> "You must thoroughly understand the business needs before you can create a useful system"(p.341).

In implying that university student records systems do not meet the needs of all their users, we are not arguing that these systems are a failure. We are arguing, however, that they often do not achieve their full potential in the provision of *all* the useful information of which they are capable, and to all those people who could make good use of it. Unfortunately, teaching is not always seen as a business need of university student records systems.

3. POST IMPLEMENTATION EVALUATION

The field of post implementation review is well researched in a number of knowledge domains. In education and health, writers such as Visscher (1999) and Perrin (2000) have written seminal articles on the value and problems associated with measuring effectiveness against specifications as opposed to using level-of-use as a post implementation review technique. A common nature of post implementation review concentrates on levels of use, of the program, or of specific functionality of the program. Visscher (1999) proposes

> "the higher the perceived system quality, the more the implementation process promotes system use, and the more the features of the SISs match the nature of schools, the more intense the use of SISs is expected to be." (p.172)

The argument here that 'if it is good it will be used, if it is used it must be good' helps us to distinguish between systems. It cannot, however, help us with the quality and purpose of a system to the extent that a system is missing features, or is ignoring some of its potential users.

In health, several researchers have identified gains to be made when clients or users are consulted directly after implementation (Osher et al. 2001; Shah 2001). In the health knowledge domain, these viewpoints have been compared, and Lee and Menon (2000) used both parametric and non-parametric analysis of the efficiencies gained by IT investment in hospitals.

Their conclusions were different from other studies in the area. They based their measurements on the proposition that

"Efficiency, when measured through post-hoc analysis, tells us how well the final mix of inputs has affected production ... " (p.103)

Clearly, even within a model as rigorous as that possible when measuring efficiency, there are disparities of outcome when alternative measurement methods are employed.

A paper by Bryce et al. (2000) describes the application of three different models to measure the outcomes of a single system change. The paper concludes that:

"This article illustrates that model selection can influence which firms are rated as the most efficient. We therefore cannot simply dismiss the decision as arbitrary." (p.511)

In the hospital setting, Osher et al. (2001) argue that

"Failing to involve family members in the process of framing analysis questions and interpreting results deprives them of the opportunity to ask additional questions of the evaluation data that may improve the overall usefulness of the evaluation". (p.70)

The argument proposed by this paper is that it is useful to ask what users need from a system rather than if they are happy with the system presented. At a meeting someone will ask 'is this a convenient time to meet?' Those at the meeting are clearly able to attend at that time. The question should also, of course, be put to interested parties who are *not* in attendance. In IT systems terms the equivalent is to ask 'are you happy with the performance of the system functions?' What should also be asked, but very seldom is asked, is 'What information do you need to perform your job, and to what extent does the system currently provide that information?'

4.   STUDY OF UNIVERSITY SYSTEMS

The research reported here commenced with the study of three universities in Victoria, Australia. Anecdotal evidence had indicated a common problem amongst academics that arose from their interactions within the university administrative systems. In initial interviews academics complained about unnecessarily duplicated work. Three examples, common to all three universities, illustrate this type of problem:
- Examination results were entered by hand on a form generated from a computer printout from the central student records database. Usually,

before transcription, these results were first printed onto paper from the academics' own student record system in an Excel spreadsheet, or something similar.

– Students enrolled in courses on a computer system by filling in paper forms. These allowed course lists to be produced, but academics could only obtain a paper copy of the course list. Individual tutorial and workshop lists were not recorded on the main student record system, but on individual PCs using whatever method the individual academics had developed.

– Academic advice including such details as checks on prerequisite courses and availability of courses in semesters required for minimum time completion were delivered to students verbally as no provision for recording these in the student records systems existed. Many of these details were recorded on paper in redundant filing systems. Important details such as student progress interview results were stored on paper in files.

Interviews with academics at the three universities showed that the simplest ITEM requirements generated by classroom needs had not crossed the minds of even senior academics, let along university administrators. Such fundamental reports as student academic history, timetable clashes between course enrolments, and performance by assessment type were not only not available, but academics were so cynical about the chances of their influencing the development of university-wide systems that they had not even considered the possibility that the student records system in any way was provided to serve their needs. During the course of this research at least three separate IT systems were set up in competition to the university ITEM system by individual departments or schools.

5. DEVELOPMENT OF THE LITMUS TEST

Research has shown (Martilla and McLean 1977) that it may be more effective for users to determine those factors they think important to the effective use of information systems. In a case study by Shah (2001), it was reported that user input raised issues such as communication between the Information Services Department and users, the speed of response of particular sections of the system and the existence of specific reports. A question arises as to the prevalence of features of a system that have importance to users, but have not been emphasised by the developers of systems.

A need became apparent for a simple method of determining if a university system had been developed after taking the academic classroom needs as a stakeholder requirement. The test would best enunciate the principle if it addressed a universal need of a classroom teacher rather than a partially administrative function that had a bearing on the classroom. The question developed after several trials was:

> *Does your system allow you, at your desk, to obtain a*
> *list of the performance of students in prerequisite*
> *course for your course?*

This question was trialed on academics from a number of universities and several different discipline areas. In each case the response from the interviewee was immediate and certain: it does not!

6.   THE RESEARCH

After the preliminary studies, a wider study was conducted to see if the particular issue identified as the Litmus Test was a useful way of identifying weaknesses in a post implementation review of university systems in different cultural and political environments. Individual academics were contacted directly in: three universities in Victoria, Australia; a university in Perth, Western Australia; a university in Queensland, Australia; the Philippines at a major private university; Indonesia at a major state university; Sweden at a modern middle-level university; England at two middle-level universities; Canada at two provincial universities; the USA at a major private university and a research university in the Netherlands.

The aim of the very specific application of the Litmus Test in these universities was to determine:
− Do academics see themselves as clients of a university administrative system?
− Can instruments be developed for post implementation review that have relevance, independent of cultural considerations?
− Is the practice of developing student administration systems with little regard for improving educational experience widespread in universities?

In eleven of the thirteen cases studied, the Litmus Test was answered in the negative. The vast majority of academics interviewed indicated that there was very little information available in any form that would enable them to tune courses on the basis of student performance or readiness. Only in two cases was information of the type related to the Litmus Test available. The interviewers reported another interesting comment by respondents: several of the respondents indicated that while the information described in the Litmus Test was not available, they could not see why an academic teacher would want that information.

Analysis was then conducted in order to find some explanation of differences in responses. The first issue investigated was the existence of two universities where Litmus Test type information was available. An intense study of the systems in each case showed that the systems were much smaller and less integrated than those typical in the other institutions studied. Enquiries found that these systems had been commissioned and written by academics working at the universities concerned. An explanation for this can be found in the background of the developer. In each case the developers were experienced teachers, and it could be that their teaching experience led them to include features of particular use to other teachers. The systems in all other universities studied were, in each case, written by various commercial organisations. It could be postulated that commercial systems would be tailored to respond to the demands of those in the university responsible for funding major software projects. An analysis of the difference between typical commercial systems and the two 'home grown' systems did, in fact, show a high level of integration with financial and state reporting functions in the commercial products. This would be consistent with the proposition that developments commissioned by the senior administrative sections of a university have resulted in systems that cater only to common high level administrative needs.

Some analysis of interviews was conducted with a view to identifying differences between universities where academics were interested in teaching-data, and those where there was no pressing interest in such data. No differences were found in size, age or general aspects of educational programs. The interviewers reported a difference in culture between the relevant groups of universities. While cultural factors are difficult to define and measure, the general opinion amongst the researchers was that universities might be thought of as being in two main streams. In the first type would be those universities built on a tradition of research and scholarship. In some cases this is consistent with government funding models that support the research priority through separate and generous research funding. In these institutions the interviewers found a smaller proportion of average senior academic workload allocated to teaching duties. The second type of institution could be categorised as teaching universities. In this type of institution teaching hours for senior academics were a larger proportion of total workload and often funding was clearly on the basis of student numbers, with research being 'subtracted' from those funds where possible. Often this type of university was one where the development of the institution was from a technical institute or polytechnic with a very strong teaching tradition.

7.   CONCLUSION

Although referring to administrative information systems in schools, Fulmer and Frank contend that while these systems have been quite effective in business-related tasks such as inventory control, personnel management, cost analysis and audit, they have been

"... far less effective at depicting the conditions of teaching and learning. ... They have not provided quality data for analysing and intervening in processes of teaching and learning." (Fulmer and Frank 1997: 122)

In an earlier ITEM paper (Tatnall and Davey 1995) we also argued that educational management systems should make more use of the 'higher levels' of information system and provide decision support and executive information facilities rather than just transaction processing. In this paper likewise, we are arguing that universities are not getting the most out of their student records systems and that more functionality is possible, particularly in the provision of information to assist classroom teachers.

From our preliminary investigations it appears that, in their teaching role, academics are not satisfied with their interactions with, and the information available to them from university student records systems. To further investigate this we have developed a simple Litmus Test that can be applied painlessly and with little effort from the academics questioned. Research in the health industry has shown that the traditional methods of post hoc analysis of IT systems often misses important information that would result in increased efficiency of the organisation. The aim of the Litmus Test is to highlight that entire areas of information provision can be ignored by ITEM developers and will never be found if the post hoc review concentrates only on those factors that were included in the specifications. In thirteen universities the Litmus Test found that an entire class of potential user of university student records systems had been ignored. Only in two places was the system supplying this information. Those two counter examples had the common factor that the systems had been written by stakeholders within the institution and hence the issue of providing educational functionality might have been presumed by the unusual nature of the development team.

More research is now needed, using the Litmus Test, to see whether this technique is useful for identifying missing functionality. This research would be useful if extended to a broader range of universities and could also be applied in other industry sectors.

REFERENCES

Bryce, C.L., Engberg, J.B. and Wholey, D.R. (2000). Comparing the Agreement Among Alternative Models in Evaluating HMO Efficiency. *Health Care Services Research* 35(2), 509-528.

Fuller, F. and William, M. (1994). *Computers and Information Processing.* Boyd & Fraser, Massachusetts.

Fulmer, C.L. and Frank, F.P. (1997). Developing Information Systems for Schools of the Future. In *Information Technology in Educational Management for the Schools of the Future.* Fung, A.C.W., Visscher, A.J., Barta, B.Z. and Teather, D.C.B. (eds). Chapman & Hall / IFIP, London.

Lawrence, D.R., Shah, H.U. and Golder, P.A. (1997). Business Users and the Information Systems Development Process. In *The Place of Information Technology in Management and Business Education.* Barta, B.Z., Tatnall, A. and Juliff, P. (eds). Chapman & Hall / IFIP, London.

Lee, B. and Menon, N.M. (2000). Information Technology Value Through Different Normative Lenses. *Journal of Management Information Systems.* 16(4), 99-119.

Lindgaard, G. (1994). *Usability Testing and System Evaluation.* Chapman & Hall, London.

Martilla, L.A. and McLean, E.R. (1977). Importance Performance Analysis. *Journal of Marketing* (January), 25-33.

Meredith, J.R. and Mantel, S.J.J. (1995). *Project Management: a Managerial Approach.* John Wiley & Sons Inc, New York.

Osher, T.W., Van Kammen, W. and Zaro, S.M. (2001). Family Participation in Evaluating Systems of Care: Family, Research and Service Systems Perspectives. *Journal of Emotional and Behavioural Disorders.* 9(1), 63-70.

Perrin, R. (2000). Fine-Tuning Information Systems to Improve Performance. *Healthcare Financial Management.* 54(5), 100-102.

Post, G.V. (1999). *Database Management Systems.* McGraw Hill, London.

Shah, S.K. (2001). Improving Information Systems Performance Through Client Value Assessment: A Case Study. *Review of Business.* 22(1/2), 37-42.

Tatnall, A. and Davey, B. (1995). Executive Information Systems in School Management: a Research Perspective. In *World Conference on Computers in Education VI. WCCE'95. Liberating the Learner.* Tinsley, J.D. and van Weert, T.J. (eds), Chapman & Hall / IFIP, London.

Visscher, A.J. and Bloemen, P.P.M. (1999). Evaluation of the Use of Computer-Assisted Management Information Systems in Dutch Schools. *Journal of Research on Computing in Education.* 32(1), 172-181.

8

PORTAL TECHNOLOGY FOR INTEGRATED, USER-CENTRIC UNIVERSITY INFORMATION SYSTEMS

Marko Bajec, Viljan Mahnič and Marjan Krisper
University of Ljubljana, Faculty of Computer & Information Science, Trzaska 25, 1000 Ljubljana,Slovenia

Abstract: The paper describes a project that was launched as the first step towards the realisation of the Information Systems (IS) strategy plan developed for the University of Ljubljana.   The strategy plan revealed many weaknesses and disadvantages of the current university IS.   One of them was the lack of the possibility to utilize e-business technology. As a response the University of Ljubljana decided to renovate the current Student records IS using a technology which seems to be very promising in developing integrated, user-centric IT solutions. In the paper, we shortly introduce the strategy plan and discuss some characteristics of the portal technology. In more detail we focus on the renovation of the Student records IS. In conclusion, we expose some difficulties that we had to deal with during the project.

Key words: University information systems, portal technology, e-business, student records

1.   INTRODUCTION

The University of Ljubljana is with its 26 member institutions the largest university in Slovenia.   It has approximately 59,000 students, more than 2,600 teaching and research personnel and about 1,250 administrative staff. According to its finances, the University of Ljubljana is a kind of *state university* funded by the Ministry of Education, Science and Sport. Its rather distinguishing characteristic is that it permits member institutions to have a great autonomy in the way of their work.   In addition, the member institutions are also financially independent, as they receive funds directly from the ministry. In the future, however, this is going to change. A number of activities will be centralised and led by the university. All the correspondence with the ministry will be coordinated centrally by the university as a whole. From then on, the university will make necessary contracts with the ministry and will be entitled and responsible for receiving and distributing funds to its members.

Another important change that is affecting the operation of the university and its member institutions is based on the new approach in developing curricula. The university is adopting the so-called *credit system*, which will allow students to choose among many courses, irrespectively of the institution where the courses are delivered. In the past, this was hardly possible, as the curricula ware rigid and only based on courses delivered at a single institution. The new curricula tend to be more flexible in this respect, which will consequently require a higher level of collaboration between the university members.

The aforementioned changes affect the university as a whole and require modifications in both university structure and operation. Consequently, this requires a redesign of the University IS (UIS) to meet the new objectives. The university responded to the expected changes and ordered the development of a strategy plan for a complete and integrated UIS. The project was started in August 2001 and was successfully finished five months later with a support of a complete university board (Krisper et al, 2001).

The strategy plan has revealed many weaknesses and problems of the current IS and proposed several solutions, including an architecture for the future UIS. To provide information at all organizational levels the architecture comprised a number of interconnected sub-systems. Some of them were required for each member institution (e.g. the Student records sub-system, Finance and accounting sub-system, Human resources sub-system, etc.), while others were supposed to support centralised activities and were therefore only expected to run at the university level or at the rector's office. According to the architecture the future UIS should be supported by a number of sub-systems, including a workflow system, data warehouse, document system and decision support system.

Another important element in the UIS architecture that drew our attention was a *portal*. When we were developing an idea of a desired UIS we realised that just having all the sub-systems developed and integrated into a working whole supported by communication infrastructure, data warehouse, document system and management system is maybe not enough. This only gives an infrastructure that holds all the information required for various users. What is missing is an appropriate and effective interface through which UIS users will be able to access the information. Not only administrative staff would require such an interface, but also students, teachers and managers expect to have a way to access the information they seek. In addition, UIS users do not want to have to search through all the systems and databases but they want to have access to the data that has been prepared for them.

For example, if I am a professor and I want to see how well the students did their examination in some course that I teach, I can use a report that is most likely provided in this regard in student records sub-system (in most cases professors still have to ask the staff to send them the report). Of course, I have to tell the system, who am I, what courses interests me etc. However, if I have been authenticated to the system, why wouldn't the system prepare this information for me? The system knows who I am and what my roles are, so it could provide me with personalised information. For example, about courses I am teaching, notices from students, etc. Moreover, the system could keep information about my requests and typical inquiries and in future provide me with an even more personalised interface.

We asked ourselves, who are typical UIS users and what they typically want from the system (in technical terms). We identified several groups of users, most notably teachers, researchers, administration staff, managers, students (current, prospective and alumni students) and interested public. Of course, they have different requirements and ideas of how the system should serve their everyday work, but there are some general features each of them needed. These are:

– To access the system from everywhere (not just from work, but also from home, conference, etc.)
– To not require a complex client software to access IS (instead they would like to use an internet browser, or even mobile phone or pocket computer)
– To access all information assets through a single entry point (they don't want to have a number of different systems, usernames, passwords, etc.)
– To get personalised information and services
– To access information and services in a secure way

Although there is no common definition of a portal, several IT professionals and companies like IBM, Delphi Group, Gartner Group, Meta Group, etc. seem to agree that these are all the features of a portal. They describe a portal as "an IT solution that provides a secure, single point of interaction with diverse information, business processes and people, personalized to a user's needs and responsibilities".

Portals are extremely popular today, not just in business but also in higher education. Today almost all universities are either developing or buying portal solutions for their needs (Cunin et al. 2002, Haselbacher 2002,

Rio et al. 2002, Shaw et al. 2002, Gartner Group 2000a). JA-SIG (Java Special Interest Group) has even started a *Portal Framework Project* in which over 20 universities have been joined with an aim to develop a free, sharable portal for institutions of higher education (Olsen 2000, Gartner Group 2000b). The use of portals in higher education has also raised interests among researchers (Looney and Lyman 2000, Eisler 2000, Woods et al. 2002, Gartner Group 2000a, etc.).

In the rest of the paper, we explain our case of developing a portal solution to satisfy students', teachers' and staff information requirements. We describe a project that has taken the first step toward realization of the UIS strategy plan.

2.   RENOVATION OF THE STUDENTS RECORDS IS

2.1   Background

At a university, the Student Records Office staff is usually responsible for all administrative tasks dealing with enrolment, examination schedules, examination records, degree records, and various statistical surveys showing student progress from year to year. In order to automate the aforementioned activities, a computer based student records IS (SRIS) was developed at the University of Ljubljana in 1994 (Mahnič and Vilfan 1995). Given the fact that the University of Ljubljana is extremely decentralized, each member institution (viz. faculty, academy or college) maintains its own IS, implemented in a local area network of personal computers sharing a common database.

Experience has shown that the system satisfies the basic needs of the Student Records Office staff, but lacks the possibility to utilize e-business technology. For example, students can enter their examination applications and requests for various official statements (e.g. a transcript of completed examinations) only from workstations within the faculty premises, but they cannot use these functions from their homes. During enrolment, they must still fill a special enrolment form instead of providing the corresponding data electronically. Similarly, teachers must inform the Student Records Office about examination dates and examination grades using special forms instead of entering the corresponding data directly in the computer database.

Considering the increasing demand for distant access of data, the new system should provide not only the administrative staff, but also students and teachers with all necessary information regarding the teaching process. Additionally, the system should simplify administrative tasks and reduce paperwork by the introduction of electronic business methods wherever appropriate. In such a way, a more efficient and better communication between all parties involved (viz. students, teachers, and administrative staff) will be achieved.

Since it has been found that the maintenance of examination schedules, examination applications, and examination results is the most critical part of the system, we decided to implement this part of the new system first, while other parts (viz. enrolment data and degree records) will be added later. Therefore, in this paper only the results of the first phase are described.

2.2 Overview of requirements specification

The Requirements Specification document (Mahnič 2001) specifies the establishment of a portal based on an Oracle database that will be customized to serve three different groups of end users, viz. teaching staff, administrative staff, and students. All functions will be accessible through World Wide Web, thus requiring only a Web browser on the user's side. Where appropriate, the same functions will also be implemented for WAP and SMS protocols.

We plan to put the new system into operation immediately after the completion of the first phase. This means that both systems, the old and the new one, will run in parallel until the old system is completely rebuilt. Therefore, special attention was devoted to the minimization of data interchange between the old database (implemented in Clipper) and the new one (implemented in Oracle). It was found that the update functions must also be included in the new system although at the beginning our intention was merely to disseminate information stored in the database. A complete list of functions considered for implementation in the first phase is shown in Table 8-1.

The F1 function enables the creation, updating and deletion of examination schedule data. At the University of Ljubljana the schedule of examinations is quite flexible, and is often subject to agreement between teachers and students. Therefore, this function is available not only to administrative staff, but to teachers as well (however, only for the subjects they teach). Each exam consists of two parts: written and oral. Functions F1 through F8 refer to the written part of examination while functions F9 to F13 deal with the oral part.

The examination schedule can be seen via the F2 function, which lists examination dates using different criteria (time period, subject etc.). F3 and F4 functions enable students to enter and cancel examination applications, respectively. The F3 function checks whether a student applied only for examinations that are on his course list as well as some other conditions (e.g.

that the total number of examination attempts is below a set maximum, that students are billed if necessary etc. etc.). Experience has shown that some teachers also accept candidates who did not apply for an examination in time. In order to deal with such exceptions, the teaching and administrative staff is given the possibility to enter an examination application after the prescribed deadline. Similarly, teaching and administrative staff can delete an application if a student was unable to attend the exam due to illness etc.

The F5 function gives teaching and administrative staff the exact numbers of candidates for each examination, while function F6 produces lists of applicants. Results of the written part of examination (together with grades of seminar work that contribute to the final grade) are entered using function F7 and students are notified using function F8.

The F9 function enables the creation, updating, and deletion of examination times for oral examination, while function F10 lists these times using different criteria (time period, teacher, subject etc.). A student can apply for oral examination only if he/she has passed the written part of the exam. This condition is checked by function F11 that enables students to enter an examination application, while function F12 cancels an existing application. The F13 function produces lists of applicants. After the oral examination, a student is given the final grade, which can be entered in the system by the examiner or administrative staff (function F14). The F15 function provides a statistical survey of examination results that enables the comparison of results in different examination periods and serves as a basis for decisions dealing with the improvements of the study process.

The F16 function provides a student a record of all exams he/she passed and grades obtained. In this, way he/she has access to all data about his/her study that are recorded in the Student Records Office. Through function F17 students can send their requests for various official statements, e.g. student transcripts (report of examinations passed), and statement of enrolment.

Finally, the F18 function gives the teaching and administrative staff the possibility to send students various messages and notifications. The most important feature of this function is the possibility to define the subset of students that will receive information according to different criteria: the academic year, year of study, study program, courses taken, manner of studies (full-time, part-time), type of enrolment (first time, repeated enrolment) etc.

Table -1. Functions to be implemented in the first phase

ID	Function Description	Teachers	Admin. Staff	Students	WEB	WAP	SMS
F1	Maintenance of examination schedules	✓	✓	✓			
F2	Survey of examination schedules	✓	✓	✓	✓	✓	
F3	Examination application	✓	✓	✓	✓	✓	
F4	Cancellation of examination application	✓	✓	✓	✓	✓	
F5	Survey of number of applications	✓	✓	✓			
F6	Lists of candidates for examination	✓	✓	✓			
F7	Entry of results of the written part of examination	✓		✓			
F8	Notification of results of the written part of an exam	✓			✓	✓	✓
F9	Maintenance of oral examination schedules	✓		✓			
F10	Survey of oral examination schedules	✓			✓	✓	
F11	Entry of an oral exam application			✓	✓	✓	
F12	Cancellation of an oral exam application			✓	✓	✓	
F13	Lists of candidates for oral examination	✓		✓			
F14	Entry of the final grade	✓	✓		✓		✓
F15	Statistical survey of examination results	✓	✓				
F16	List of passed exams		✓	✓	✓		
F17	Requests for various official statements			✓	✓	✓	
F18	Messages to students:				✓	✓	✓
	send	✓	✓				
	receive			✓			

3. PROBLEMS AND EXPERIENCES

The biggest problem that we were facing during the project initiation was how to cover all the specifics of the 26 member institutions that all but one claim to need a new system as soon as possible. Being aware that not all members could be covered in a single big step, we decided to establish a group of pilot institutions. It would be probably better if we had divided the members into groups of similar requirements and structure and then taken representatives. Unfortunately, this was not possible, since almost any institution had some specifics.

According to the aforementioned strategy plan, the university was expected to develop a single SRIS that would be then installed and used by all the members. But the problem was that in our estimations, such a project would take at least two years, which was simply too long for the majority of university members. We realized that if we had started the development of a common system, we would have taken a chance that the institutions would go their own way developing their own SRIS. In this case, it would be rather difficult to ensure the university would be able to collect all the information that is needed for its processes. Taking into account the doubts and hesitations the university decided for the following steps:

– Firstly, a minimal set of common standards for SRIS have to be developed. The standards must include: a list of core functions the SRIS must support, a common data model (the entities that are required to support the core functions plus entities required to integrate the SRIS with other systems), and a common architecture that will ensure the system stability, security and performance.
– Once the common standards are developed, the implementation of the core functions can be outsourced to several development teams that would than develop SRISs in parallel.

Another major problem was system maintenance. Although the University of Ljubljana has a special organization unit called the University Computer Centre (UCC), which is responsible for UIS administration, maintenance and development, it did not have a good reputation. The unit is simply not capable to cover all the institutions. We must say that the University did not decide yet how it would resolve this problem. As we see the problem, it seems reasonable that each development team that develops a SRIS takes also responsibility for the system maintenance. In this way, the UCC would only need to take care for smaller interventions.

4.   CONCLUSIONS

Modernization of administrative procedures by introducing *e-business* is necessary for contemporary universities. At the University of Ljubljana we decided to rebuild the existing SRIS using a portal technology, which seems to be today one of the most promising concepts for developing integrated, user-centric IT solutions. In this paper we have briefly introduced the strategy plan that had led into the renovation of SRIS. The renovation was then described in more detail. At the end, we exposed some difficulties that we had to deal with during the project.

REFERENCES

Cunin, P.Y., Lacombe, C., Desnos, J.F. & Lenne, C. (2002). The Portal of "GreCO-Universités". In *The Changing Universities: The Challenge of New Technologies – Proceedings of the EUNIS'2002 Conference*, Santos, J.M. & Ribeiro, L.M. (ed.), Portugal June.(2002).

Eisler, D. (2000). The Portal's Progress: A Gateway for Access, Information, and Learning Communities, *Syllabus Magazine*, 14(1).
http://www.syllabus.com/syllabusmagazine/sept00_fea.html.

Gartner Group (2000a). *Higher Education Enterprise Portals. Gartner Group Research Note, SPA-11-0354*

Gartner Group (2000b). *JA-SIG's Community-Sourced Portal for Higher Education. Gartner Group Research Note, P-11-9781*

Haselbacher, F. (2002). Design and operation of a WEB-databased university-information-management-system. In *The Changing Universities: The Challenge of New Technologies – Proceedings of the EUNIS'2002 Conference*, Santos, J.M. & Ribeiro, L.M. (ed.), Portugal, June, 2002.

Krisper, M., Bajec, M., Rupnik, R., Mahnič, V., Rožanec, A., Jaklič, J., Štemberger, M. & Groznik, A. (2001). *Information System Strategy Plan for the University of Ljubljana*, University of Ljubljana, Faculty of Computer and Information Science.

Looney, M., & Lyman, P. (2000)- Portals in Higher Education: What are they, and what is their potential? *EDUCAUSE Review*, July/August, pp. 28-35

Mahnic, V. & Vilfan, B (1995). Design of the Student Records Information System at the Univeristy of Ljubljana, In *Trends in Academic Information systems in Europe - Conference Proceedings*, J. Knop (ed.), Heinrich-Heine-Universität, Düsseldorf, Germany, November,1995.

Mahnic, V. (2001). *Requirements Specification for the first phase of the E-student project*, University of Ljubljana, Faculty of Computer and Information Science.

Olsen, F. (2000). Institutions Collaborate on Development of Free Portal Software, *The Chronicle of Higher Education, Information Technology*, 5, May.

Río, J., Taboada, J.A., Flores, J. & Gómez-Sobradelo, M.V. (2002) Design of a web-based MIS for the USC using multiple data sources. In *The Changing Universities: The Challenge of New Technologies – Proceedings of the EUNIS'2002 Conference*, Santos, J.M. & Ribeiro, L.M. (ed.), Portugal, June, 2002.

Shaw, T., Strachan, A., McCauley, G. & McCrae, L. (2002). The portal as the framework for the information strategy? In *The Changing Universities: The Challenge of New Technologies – Proceedings of the EUNIS'2002 Conference*, Santos, J.M. & Ribeiro, L.M. (ed.), Portugal, June, 2002.

Woods, K., Boice, M. & Hudson, M. (2002). The Evolution of the Digital Campus. In *The Changing Universities: The Challenge of New Technologies – Proceedings of the EUNIS'2002 Conference*, Santos, J.M. & Ribeiro, L.M. (ed.), Portugal, June,2002.

SECTION 3

THE MANAGEMENT OF E-LEARNING

9

FOSTERING WEB BASED TEACHING AND LEARNING IN A UNIVERSITY
Some preliminary findings at Hong Kong Baptist University

Alex Fung and Jenilyn Ledesma
Faculty of Social Sciences, Hong Kong Baptist University, Hong Kong, China

Abstract: The information revolution of the last 20 years has transformed society, business and culture, placing pre-eminence on the ability to access and use information. Such a trend continues at an incredibly accelerating pace, which makes it a big challenge for educators to keep up with. Like many universities in Hong Kong and elsewhere, Hong Kong Baptist University (HKBU) is rapidly expanding its use of information technology for teaching and learning. A Taskforce was set up to promote web based teaching and learning activities within the university community. This paper reports some preliminary findings on the nature, approach and progress made by the Taskforce during its first phase of implementation of the WebCT – the current platform for the initiative. A survey conducted by the Taskforce found that academics showed a strong desire for training and workshops, and the need of resource personnel to support their use of technology in teaching. Academics also expressed the importance of having sufficient time to learn to use the WebCT and to prepare contents, and they value opportunities to interact with colleagues for sharing experiences. Despite limited resources, the feedback on the promotion of WebCT for the teaching and learning processes at HKBU was found to be quite positive in the initial phase. The activities of the Taskforce are now into its second phase of implementation. Apart from the training and workshop support provided, the Taskforce will also look into the pedagogical impact of this initiative to staff and students alike. This should shed information on how to help academics and students adjust and prosper in a changing educational climate, and eventually on contributing to the development of a culture which recognizes and values the use of IT in education.

Key words: WebCT, web based teaching and learning, higher education

1.   INTRODUCTION

"...., we believe that the innovative application of... C&IT holds out much promise for improving the quality, flexibility and effectiveness of higher education. The potential benefits will extend to, and affect the practice of, learning and teaching and research." (Dearing Report, 1997: 13.1).

Academics have used e-mail to communicate with each other since the early 1980s. With the recent growth of the World Wide Web (WWW) and the explosion of the Internet, many lecturers and academic departments have started exploiting the potential of these technologies and the sophisticated network infrastructure to enhance their teaching. Increasing numbers of teaching staff are beginning to put their lecture notes and reading materials on the web for students to browse and use. They have also started communicating with their students via email.

Course outlines are commonly published on departmental websites. Some university libraries have web-interfaces for searching, checking availability and reserving books. Conferencing software is used in some institutions to create on-line discussion groups amongst students. These simple innovations are only the beginning, and it is not surprising to find a recent wave of interest amongst software developers and IT research groups within universities in exploring ways to further leverage technology in an educational context. Against the background of changes in Higher Education required to achieve the vision of 'a learning society' painted by the Dearing Report (1997) in the UK, which is also a factor in the current Education Reform in Hong Kong, this study focuses on the development of web based teaching and learning initiative at Hong Kong Baptist University.

2.   BACKGROUND

2.1   Origin

This section provides information about how and why the use of web based learning environments for teaching and learning at HKBU was developed, in addition to the context, scope and boundaries that define its scale. This initiative stemmed from a pilot project carried out by the Faculty of Social Sciences in 1999-2001, which was built upon the work (related to web based teaching and learning) that already started at HKBU such as the WebCH – an in-house developed system for subject web page construction.

The pilot project adopted WebCT[5] as the platform to systematically support the development of web based and web-assisted teaching and learning within the Faculty.

The positive response from lecturers and students participating in the pilot project subsequently led the senior management of HKBU to increase its scope to a university-wide level. As a result, the Academic and Professional Standards Committee (APSC) set up a Web based Teaching and Learning Taskforce in July 2001 to promote the use of the technology to enhance teaching and learning quality, using WebCT as an initial platform. The Taskforce was established to spearhead the University onto a greater use of IT platforms in the conduct of teaching and learning, and was entrusted with the responsibility for devising a strategic plan for promoting the development of web based teaching and learning in the university community. The Taskforce was formed to serve a two-year term. An overview of the initiative, including its conduct and those involved, is presented in the following section.

2.2   Overview

Memberships for the Taskforce were drawn up from different faculties, along with the terms of reference, by the APSC. The University provided funding for the equipment, the WebCT license, and a small support team of three personnel for the operation of the Taskforce. During the first few months of implementation in the 1st semester of academic year 2001-02, the primary focus of the Taskforce was to provide WebCT training and workshops to interested teaching and non-teaching staffs. The Taskforce also created a homepage to provide information and reference to users, with materials not only on WebCT and its training, but covering web based teaching and learning in general. A user survey was conducted at the end of the 1st semester, covering all full-time academic staff, to collect feedback on the WebCT initiative.

2.3   Aims

The new forces of globalisation, rapid growth in IT capacity, changing patterns and demands on education all interact in ways that are transforming the character and structure of tertiary education (Biggs, 1999; Brennan & Shah, 2000). HKBU, like any other university, is also rapidly expanding its use of web based technologies to enhance teaching and learning. The broad aim of this initiative was to promote a web based teaching and learning

---

[5] WebCT is the Web Course Tool available from www.WebCT.com

culture in the university community. The more specific aim of the current initiative was on the pedagogical applications of these technologies, in particular maintaining quality while increasing effectiveness and efficiency in teaching and learning. As higher education continues to embrace these new technologies, the need for academics to evaluate the impact of this paradigm shift magnifies.

3.   PROCEDURAL OPERATION

3.1   Scope

It is necessary to clarify several aspects of the initiative's focus and signal some limitations on its scope. The Taskforce's starting point is to achieve a critical mass of WebCT users, hopefully to contribute to and positively influence teaching and learning practices. Secondly, the process of 'operation' involves the exercise of a steering role by the Chairman of the Taskforce and the overarching advisory role by the Advisory members of the Taskforce.

The limitation of this initiative is two-fold. First, the budget allocated for the initiative is quite scarce, making it difficult if not impossible for the Taskforce to speed up the engagement of the academic staff on using WebCT for teaching and learning. Secondly, WebCT is seen as a system requiring further development rather than a 'perfect system'. The initiative is expected to continue to evolve in response to the rapidly changing context, and to the nature of teaching and learning paradigm shifts in higher education. Thus, it is as effective as possible to add value to 'what is already there' by remaining open to adaptation to 'what might be'.

3.2   Approach

The Taskforce had two approaches.

The first approach concentrates on User Training and Support for WebCT. The Taskforce aims to promote WebCT usage by conducting comprehensive training and workshops of different levels at regular intervals. Academic and non-academic, staff including technicians and support staff from various disciplines, are encouraged to participate. A Help Desk has been set up to provide technical support.

The second approach addresses the pedagogical issues associated with the use of technology for teaching and learning. Seminars to promote the use of WebCT for teaching and learning, and the integration of pedagogy and practice are organized. Updated and relevant information on web based teaching and learning are made available on the website. Consultations with colleagues, surveys and other related studies are carried out to provide references for best practices and informed decision-making by the Taskforce in its development of the strategic plan to be submitted to the Senate via APSC at the end of its 2-year term.

3.3   Operation

The development of the initiative aimed to create a geographically dispersed user community at HKBU. While its use is optional, the overall approach of the project focused on the achievement of university-wide outcomes. Even at the early phase of the initiative, progress towards this outcome already required the establishment of collaborations with discipline-specific academic staff, as well as the identification of a pool of WebCT users to provide support and share similar experiences.

Despite the very limited budget and resources, the development of the initiative has encouraged academic staff in adapting to and utilizing the new web based resources. The operation of the support team, albeit small, also offered significant help for academics, particularly to those who are new and wanting to explore what is available for them. The quality of feedback adds incalculable confidence to the Taskforce.

4.   PROGRESS AND OUTCOMES

4.1   Milestones

The following were some of the key milestones in the development of the initiative:
– establishment of the Taskforce and its membership
– consultation meetings with the Taskforce advisory team members
– employment of support team personnel
– relatively standard literature search on related topics
– establishment of the web page (WebCT and the Taskforce)
– development of training materials
– delivery of workshops / training to academic and non-academic staff
– identification of staff needs for professional development in this aspect (via survey questionnaire)

4.2   Needs Analysis

Using a self-developed instrument, a needs assessment survey was administered conducted to all 400 full time academic staff. The primary purpose of the survey was to collect feedback on what are (if any) the needs they deemed as necessary for the ease of use in performing various tasks associated with web based teaching and learning. Another purpose of the survey was also to find out the existing profile of academics in terms of using information technology for teaching and learning.

In the survey, respondents were asked to describe any web based systems that they were using for teaching and learning prior to the Taskforce formation. In particular, they were asked for details of the use of computers, virtual learning environments, and the World Wide Web. Another part of the instrument surveyed respondents on their awareness of the activities carried out by the Taskforce, as well as its level of effectiveness in serving their needs.

4.2.1   Background of the respondents

37.7% (n=26) of the respondents have been teaching at HKBU for 1-5 years, while another 20.3% (n=14) taught for 6-10 years. There was an equal proportion of academic staff that taught for less than a year (n=11, 15.9%) and 11-15 years (n=11, 15.9%). Only 8.7% (n=6) taught for more than 15 years at HKBU. The respondents were broken down into different faculties, as shown in Table 9-1 below.

Table 9-1. Responses by Faculty

Faculty	Number of Responses	Percentage
Arts	22	31.9%
Business	9	13.0%
Communication	4	5.8%
Science	12	17.4%
Chinese Medicine	1	1.4%
Continuing Education	11	15.9%
Social Sciences	8	11.6%

4.2.2   Response rate

A total of 400 questionnaires were sent out to all full time academic staff. 69 valid responses were collected; the response rate was 17.25%. Phone follow-ups were made to increase the response rate. The cut-off date was also extended from 2 to 4 weeks to allow more time for academic staff to return the answered questionnaire.

The number of survey forms returned was unfortunately too low to warrant detailed analysis of the results. Hence, the conclusions drawn from these results were not representative of the HKBU academic community. Some possible reasons that might account for the low rate of return other than simple lack of willingness or time to participate were:

- The time of the survey implementation coincided with the examination period of HKBU. As a consequence, the majority of the academic staff were occupied with the preparation and marking of the examination results.
- The time of the survey implementation was near the Christmas holidays. The majority of them went on holidays right after the examination period, leaving little or almost no time to respond to the survey questionnaires.
- The surveys were sent to academic staff via departmental secretaries. It is possible that they might not know about the survey being implemented. Lack of coordination at the departmental level may be one explanation for the low response rate.
- The use of web based approaches to teaching and learning is still embryonic at this stage. Hence, the level of interest and awareness of academic staff to alternative teaching / learning methods may also be another factor.

4.3 Some highlights from the findings

This section is divided into three parts. The first part provides a picture of the HKBU academic staff profile on IT use for teaching and learning. Part 2 gives an account of the degree of awareness (of HKBU academic staff) of the Taskforce and its associated activities. The last part, Part 3, indicates the preparation and development needs as perceived by the HKBU academic staff.

4.3.1 Profile of HKBU academic staff on IT use for teaching and learning

IT literacy and usage. Before the start of the 2001-2002 academic year, more than half of the respondents (n=45, 65.2%) have been using computers for more than 10 years. Another quarter (n=18, 26.1%) were also using computers for at least 5 years or more. However, most of the computer usage related only to word processing (frequent: n=66, 95.7%) and presentation (sometimes to frequent: n=39, 56.5%). Only 4 of the respondents were using computers for other reasons like faxing, video and image editing, programme authoring for teaching and research, and programming. In terms of training, more than half of the respondents (n=36,

52.2%) did not attend any IT courses during the past academic year 2000-2001. Only 33.3% (n=23) had between 1-3 IT training courses, whilst another 10.1% (n=7) attended at least 4-6. Only 2.9% (n=2) had 10 or more IT training courses in the past academic year 2000-2001.

IT in teaching and learning. Prior to 2001-2002 academic year, only 36.2% (n=25) were adopting some form of web based teaching prior the 2001-2002 academic year. Slightly more than half of the respondents (n=14, 56.0%) were using WebCH, a platform developed internally by the Academic Registry of HKBU. Another 28.0% (n=7) were using self-developed homepages, while only 20.0% (n=5) were WebCT users. A small proportion used self-made web based programmes; others used Macromedia software packages for interactive teaching objectives and platforms provided by other faculties (i.e. Social Sciences) and other universities (i.e. Hong Kong Polytechnic University Language Teaching website).

During the first semester of the academic year 2001-2002, more than half (n=44, 63.8%) were not using WebCT for teaching and learning. Of those using WebCT, 13 (18.8%) used it for 2 subjects. Another 5 (7.2%) used it for at least 1 subject, while only 2 (2.9%) used it for 3 subjects or more. Some staff members also used platforms other than WebCT, such as WebCH, self-developed homepages, or platforms provided by other faculties (such as the Social Sciences) or other institutions (such as PolyU Language Teaching website).

The WebCT usage summary at the end of the first semester 2001-2002 (i.e. 31st December 2001) was calculated as follows in Table 9-2:

Table 9-2. WebCT usage summary* This figure includes full time and part time academic staff

Faculty	N	%
BUS: School of Business	25 out of 67	25.4%
SCI: Faculty of Science	15 out of 122	12.3%
SOSC: Faculty of Social Sciences	35 out of 195	18.0%
ARTS: Faculty of Arts	6 out of 159	3.8%
COMM: School of Communication	N	16.0%
SCM: School of Chinese Medicine	25 out of 67	10.0%
TOTAL	15 out of 122	14.8%

When the academic staff were asked whether they have an intention to use WebCT for teaching and learning in the second semester of the academic year 2001-2002, only 27.5% (n=19) and 17.4% (n=12) intend to use it for 1 and 2 different subjects respectively. Slightly less than half (n=33, 47.8%) indicated no intention of using WebCT in the second semester of the academic year 2001-2002.

Preferred approach for IT use. The academic staff members were also asked for their most preferred approach when using web based technology to support teaching and learning (Table 9-3). Majority of the respondents opted for level 4 (learning on their own, with access to technical support when needed), and level 1 (having technical support to prepare the materials). There was an equal preference for levels 2 and 3 (work with mixed team, and learning to learn without support).

Table 9-3. Preferred approaches when using web based technologies.

Level	Description	Preference			
		Least preferred	Preferred	Strongly preferred	Don't know
4	Learn the technology skills so that I can prepare materials myself, with access to skilled technical staff when the need arises	4 (5.8%)	18 (26.1%)	**40** (58.0%)	2 (2.9%)
1	Work with skilled technical staff who will prepare the content materials based on my needs	14 (20.3%)	12 (17.4%)	**29** (42.0%)	4 (5.8%)
2	Work in a team with colleagues, including a mix of academic and technical staff, on preparing the content materials	20 (29.0%)	20 (29.0%)	**8** (11.6%)	10 (14.5%)
3	Learn on my own when the need arises without any formal instruction and support	23 (33.3%)	22 (31.9%)	**8** (11.6%)	4 (5.8%)

4.3.2 Degree of awareness on the administration and support provided by the Taskforce

Degree of awareness. 82.6% (n=57) and 73.9% (n=51) of the respondents were aware of the WebCT platform and the Web based Teaching and Learning (WebTL) Taskforce respectively. 91.3% (n=63) were also aware of the WebCT training and workshops provided by the Taskforce. However, when asked about the support provided by the Taskforce, only 65.2% (n=45) were aware of the Support Team, 52.2% (n=36) for the Help Desk, and 40.6% (n=28) for the WebTL Website. In fact, only 33.3% (n=23) has sought for support from the Support Team / Help Desk.

Channel for obtaining information. The most popular source of learning about the WebTL Taskforce and its associated activities was through the Email message system of HKBU (i.e. Postman). This accounted for 88.4%

(n=61). The next sources of information channel were through colleagues and friends (n=24, 34.8%) and direct mail posting (n=21, 30.4%), followed by the HKBU website (n=9, 13.0%). The WebTL and WebCT websites were the least popular channels for obtaining information about the activities of the Taskforce.   This accounted for 1.4% (n=1) and 8.7% (n=6) respectively.

Workshops offered. Of the 69 respondents, only 25 (36.2%) attended the WebCT workshops offered by the Taskforce. The majority of them rated the overall quality of the workshops as acceptable (n=12, 48.0%) to above average (n=10, 40.0%).   The respondents also expressed that the most convenient time to offer these workshops (in the future) was on Monday (n=12, 17.4%) and Tuesday afternoons (n=7, 10.1%).   Another 7 (10.1%) also expressed Friday afternoon as a possible timeslot.

4.3.3   Preparation and development needs of HKBU academic staff

Academic staff members were asked to feedback on what are (if any) their needs for the preparation and development of skills necessary in performing various tasks associated with web based teaching and learning. They were also asked to comment on the hindering factors that could have affected their progress. Table 9-4, below, shows the needs expressed by the respondents, in order of priority.

Table 9-4. Pre-requisites for using WebCT

Preparation and Development Needs	N	%
Face to face training and workshops of different types in the use of WebCT	39	56.5%
One on one personal consultations to use WebCT	25	36.2%
Departmental local support for WebCT	25	36.2%
On-line self access learning to use WebCT	24	34.8%
Department based training, workshop, experience sharing to use WebCT	24	34.8%
CD-ROMS on how to use WebCT	13	18.8%
University wide experience sharing sessions on using WebCT	7	10.1%
Centralised WebCT content development support	3	4.3%

One interesting finding from the survey showed that more than half of the respondents (n=45, 65.2%) did not think incentives were needed for staff members who use web based technology to enhance teaching and learning. At the time of this reporting, the Taskforce has already started looking into this issue.

When asked what conditions prevent or limit the use of WebCT in teaching, the following responses were given by the respondents (Table 9-5).

Table 9-5. Inhibitors to WebCT use

Conditions that prevent or limit WebCT use	N	%
Not enough time to develop content materials for WebCT	41	59.4%
Not enough time to attend WebCT training and workshops	36	52.2%
Still learning the knowledge and skills of using WebCT for instruction	21	30.4%
Unsure whether the use of web based technology is beneficial to students	17	24.6%
Classroom infrastructure is inappropriate for web based teaching	17	24.6%
Insufficient provision of technical support	10	14.5%
Lack of personal interest to use WebCT	9	13.0%
Not ready to change my existing teaching strategies	8	11.6%
Lack of content development support	8	11.6%
WebCT not user friendly enough	7	10.1%
Unsure whether the use of web based technology is beneficial to self	7	10.1%
Prefers using other instructional software to help meet learning objectives	6	8.7%
Students' attitudes are not ready for web based learning	4	5.8%
Insufficient training and workshops	4	5.8%
Need for departmental policy / leadership	4	5.8%
Not ready to change my teaching role	2	2.9%

Others also expressed lack of time, lack of expertise/knowledge, and lack of support (i.e. helper to design WebCT materials) as hindrances for WebCT use. Some of the other reasons provided were:

- 'A lot of WebCT is irrelevant to the way I do things, and it's very cumbersome'.
- 'It can only be used when semester is about to start, I can't prepare in advance'.
- 'Difficulty in presenting graphics of chemical structure or mathematical equation in a text based system like WebCT'.
- 'Manual of WebCT is not good'.
- 'No need to use it'.
- 'Some students do not participate in WebCT'.
- 'Students may not be able to access it'.
- 'Not all students have computers at home, the access to Internet is slow'.
- 'Time consuming'.
- 'Self-developed website is being used'.
- 'WebCT does not provide the design freedom needed for my class'.

5.   DISCUSSION

The development of high performance computing and communications has resulted in the production of new media, such as the Web and virtual realities. These new types of messages and experiences have transformed traditional instruction based only on classroom learning into a broader and potentially more powerful repertoire of pedagogical strategies.

There are a number of points raised by this paper which shed lights on what academic staff at HKBU need to support their use of web based technologies for teaching and learning. The single most important conclusion reached is that the potential benefit of information technology can be realized provided careful attention is paid to a range of factors, including:

– appropriate attention to the context into which the new initiative is being introduced;
– provision of an appropriate organizational infrastructure; and
– motivating academic staff and students in using IT to enhance teaching and learning practices.

This paper provides a snapshot of the progress made by HKBU on its undertaking towards web based teaching and learning practices in the university community. This is only the first phase of a two-year term. The Taskforce at this stage will continue to promote WebCT and ensure that it is fully integrated into the teaching and learning practice. Training and workshops will also be offered on a regular basis. Strategies on achieving better forms of teaching and learning will be looked at. While many universities are still experimenting with teaching and learning in electronic environments, it is important to note that this experimentation requires institutional support to ensure continual success. This is the direction that the Taskforce will continue to thrive beyond its initial phase, with a set of recommendations to be drawn up linking changes at the macro level of systems and polices of higher education, to changes at the micro level concerned with curricula, teaching, learning and assessment.

REFERENCES

Biggs, J. (1999). *Teaching for Quality Learning at University*. Society for Research into Higher Education and Open University Press, Buckingham, UK.
Brennan, J. and Shah, T. (2000). *Managing Quality in Higher Education: An International Perspective on Institutional Assessment and Change*. Open University Press, Philadelphia, PA.

The National Committee Of Inquiry Into Higher Education (1997). *Higher Education In The Learning Society: The Dearing Report.* HMSO Copyright Unit, St. Clements House, 2-16 Colegate, Norwich NR3 1BQ.

10

LEARNER AND COURSE INTEROPERABILITY IN A WEB BASED TRAINING MODEL

Rima Abdallah[1], Abdelmalek Benzekri[2], Ali El Hajj[3] and Ibrahim Moukarzel[4]

1 Institut de Recherche en Informatique de Toulouse (IRIT), Université Paul Sabatier (UPS) - Toulouse, France. (A collaboration with American University of Bierut, Co-Tutelle UPS – Université Libanaise (UL))
2 IRIT, UPS - Toulouse, France
3 Department of Electrical and Computer Engineering, Faculty of Engineering and Architecture, American University of Beirut, PO Box 11-0236 Beirut, Lebanon
4 Faculté de Genie, UPS

Abstract: Learning Management Systems (LMS) are widely used by educational institutions. Their drawback is the lack of flexibility in sharing and exchanging learning resources and learner data. In this paper, a new Web Based Training/Education (WBT/E) Model based on the Learning Technology Systems Architecture (LTSA) standard and on the WBT Model of the Enhance Project will be presented. It is hoped that this model overcomes the reusability and interoperability problems at the learner and course level. For illustration, a scenario of collaborative learning stakeholders perspective will be presented. In this scenario, WebCT will be used as the distance-learning platform, RealNetworks family for manipulating synchronized multimedia courses integrated in WebCT, and Microsoft NetMeeting for providing audio/video/sharing of application between users.

Key words: Web based training, e-learning, e-learning standard, WebCT

1.   INTRODUCTION

Nowadays, learning Management Systems (LMS) have gained interest for their wide use by educational institutions.   Moreover, the future framework of LMS will provide interchange with legacy systems via e-commerce transaction.   Therefore, these systems must meet requirements such as accessibility, flexibility, extensibility, reusability, interoperability, scalability, and security (Harvi 2000).   However, reusability and interoperability has not been well addressed by many of these systems. For example, learner information on an LMS cannot be re-used on another LMS due to the absence of standards.   In recent years, an effort was made to develop e-learning standards by several organizations such as IEEE (Institute of Electrical and Electronic Engineers) Learning Technology Standards Committee (LTSC), IMS and others.   (An exhaustive list of these can be found in ISO 2002; Robson 2000; and Babu 2001).

In this paper, a new Web Based Training/Education (WBT/E) Model will be presented.   This model is mainly based on the Learning Technology Systems Architecture (LTSA) standard IEEE and on the WBT Model of the Enhance Project (Enhance, Benzekri et al. 2002).   It identifies the requirements and components of e-learning systems, and we believe it overcomes the reusability and interoperability problems at the learner and course level.   This is done by incorporating in this model the standards developed by the IEEE 1484 LTSC.   This includes the IEEE PAPI for learner profiles and IEEE CMI (Course Management Interchange) for the developed course.   Moreover, this model leads to a reduced course production cost, quality improvement, larger potential market, and life long learning improvement.

For illustration, a scenario of collaborative learning stakeholder's perspective will be presented.   In this scenario, WebCT will be used as the distance-learning platform, RealNetworks family for manipulating synchronized multimedia courses integrated in WebCT.   Microsoft NetMeeting will be embedded into WebCT to facilitate audio/video/sharing of applications between users.

In this paper, The LTSA framework and the Enhance model are presented in section 2.   The new model is introduced in section 3 and illustrated in section 4.   Concluding remarks are given in section 5.

2.   THE LTSA FRAMEWORK AND THE ENHANCE MODEL

The IEEE LTSA framework is the standard for learning technology systems architecture, developed by IEEE LTSC. This framework consists of five layers (IEEE)

1. The first layer (highest) represents the learner/environment interaction. It provides a one-way flow of information from the environment to the learner entity.
2. Layer 2 is the learner related design feature. It is used to identify learners' influence on the design of the architecture, which helps in the selection of the needed lower layer components.
3. Layer 3 identifies the LTSA system components that include four processes, two stores, and thirteen data and control information flows.
4. Layer 4 identifies the LTSA components subsets that will be emphasized and de-emphasized according to the learning technology stakeholder's perspectives.
5. Layer 5 provides all the interoperable components such as Application Program Interface (APIs), Coding, and Protocols, as identified in the upper layer. This allows application portability, data portability, and wide area end-to-end interoperability.

"Enhance" is a European Aeronautical Industry whose objective is the increase of awareness in concurrent engineering techniques, and the improvement of training processes and methods in the aeronautical industry. The Enhance WBT/E Model is organized in eight concepts:

1. The Organization concept discusses the general organization and various structure of the platform. Moreover, it discusses the personalized training, the objectivist and constructivist type of learning with the various interactions. It also identifies the various roles, administration, and databases in a WBT/E platform.
2. The user interface concept provides the various tools to the role player depending on the task.
3. The communication concept identifies the communication between platform users using different synchronous/asynchronous audio/video/textual/graphical tools in public/private. It discusses also the communication between users and the platform itself.
4. The tracking concept specifies the user and course tracking features.
5. The evaluation concept identifies the methods for grading, testing, certification, and final examination.
6. The course structure concept is defined to guarantee an easy integration and re-use of course documents. Hence, it identified a hierarchical course

structure that is composed of modules. A module consists of a set of learning units, and each learning unit consists of didactic objects.

7. The course development concept provides a common methodology of five steps that takes into consideration the knowledge level to enhance the reusability of resources at the various steps.

8. The network concept identifies the security features such as integrity, confidentiality and authentication. In addition, it presents the various platform access principles, access technology, and the network QoS etc.

These eight concepts map to the components of Layer 3 while adding additional details. It follows that LTSA embraces the Enhance model at a high level without providing a high degree of details. The Enhance model can therefore be considered as a WBT/E illustration of implementation that conforms to and map to the LTSA architecture.

3.   THE IMPROVED MODEL

The future framework of LMS will become the central part of a Global system that will provide quick and cost effective integration with legacy systems for the exchange of interoperable learner information and developed courses. Therefore, it will allow the knowledge capitalization of high quality developed courses integrated in KMS and remote repositories over the Internet. In addition, it will provide the management of human resources in ERP applications that include the acquired competences and qualifications by the learner through a follow up of his entire path over the curriculum. Hence, any other learner will get the same expertise if he/she follows the same path over the courses of the curriculum. Moreover, it will be used for worldwide recruitment since it will provide information on the most competent expert in any field.

In this section, a new Web Based Training/Learning model for LMS will be presented. This model is based on the LTSA architecture. It includes all Enhance model concepts and adds interoperability at the learner and course level. This is achieved by standardizing database design and data structures. This model has components, it adds requirements for an open system, and provides interoperability:

- Model Components: The model components are the same as LTSA architecture layer 3 components: processes, stores, data, and control flow components. The details of their implementation are defined in the Enhance model.
- Model Requirements: The model describes an e-learning open system. This requires features such as accessibility, nomadicity, flexibility, extensibility, reusability, interoperability, scalability, availability, security,

e-commerce (Harvi 2000). It also supports personalized, collaborative, objectivist, and constructivist learning synchronously with a multicasting media delivery or asynchronously with a unicasting media delivery while using the cross platform Internet browser.

– Interoperability: Three interoperability components are defined in LTSA. These components are API, protocols, and codings. It is suggested in this model the addition of database design and data structures.

Interoperability and Reusability at the learner level are possible by adding standard learner profiles that contain the major information to be interchanged between e-learning systems. The IEEE 1484.1 Learner Model could be used. It is composed of six categories of information that can be grouped together in one database or separated in six databases linked together with a standard learner identifier. These categories of information are the learner Personal information, learners' relations information, learner security information, learner performance, and learner portfolio information. This information will have several advantages such as providing the necessary details for a personalized training. Moreover, we suggest the use of a local standard learner identifier that points to a global standard learner identifier (Benzekri et al. 2001). In this way, learner data can be exchanged by various LMS.

Interoperability and Reusability at the course level is possible by using a standard database with standard course structure. We suggest the use of the IEEE 1484.11 CMI standard (IEEE) that also applies to LMS. This will define a standard course structure that is based on a hierarchical data structure. Each course is composed of a grouping of Assignable Units (AU) and other blocks in an order implied in a list or explicit using the prerequisite. Each AU may include course introduction, tests, lessons, course summary etc. Each level in the hierarchy can be indexed by standard metadata. The separation between the course structure from the course content is conceptually very important for the reusability of independent learning content. In addition, the LMS will be responsible for controlling the sequencing of the course content which is defined in the IEEE CMI course structure. The course content will be composed of instructional elements that are based on common templates and hierarchical object models (Abdallah et al. 2002c). This hierarchical objects Model will be based on the IMS-QTI in the case of test AU (Abdallah et al. 2002b) and on the MPEG-4 (2002) in the case of media AU (Abdallah et al. 2002c). Moreover, the MPEG-7 Media content description MPEG-7 (2002) will be used to describe the media object and AU (Abdallah et al. 2002c).

Our objective is to populate the LMS with interoperable courseware and use of interoperable learner profile to exchange the information with other remote legacy and operational systems. LMS should have complete and detailed tracking, together with the information (such as competencies, certifications) stored in the learner model, which will provide the pedagogical baseline for building adaptive and intelligent type of learning. Hence, it will determine what the student should next experience. For this, LMS should track all user interaction, activities, performance, and monitor the progress and performance over the content. This will require a standard communication model of the information being exchanged between learning resources and LMS. For example this will inform the instructor that the student has really passed over all the steps at least once which is not possible to be detected with any standard classroom. As a result, all event/time object based tracking are needed.

4.   ILLUSTRATIVE EXAMPLE

In this part, an implementation of the new developed Model will be presented using the collaboration and asynchronous learning stakeholder perspective. It emphasizes the collaboration among the learners that represent the collective learner entity, the development and delivery of a multimedia presentation, the protocols, and format of multimedia flow component etc. E-learning platform WebCT (WebCT) committed to IMS and Sharable Content Object Reference Model (SCORM) standard will be used. This platform contains a learner database, course database, evaluation, delivery, multimedia, learner entity, coach, and flows. It does not support multimedia development, synchronization, and audio/video synchronous communication. To overcome these problems (Abdallah et al. 2001, Abdallah et al. 2002a), the following tools were used:

RealNetworks: RealProducer and RealPresenter were used to develop multimedia presentations. RealServer was also used to host, synchronize, and stream the multimedia presentation. Finally, the RealPlayer plug-in is integrated in WebCT courses to play the media file (Abdallah et al. 2002).

Netmeeting: H.323 Microsoft Netmeeting was embedded in WebCT courses to allow audio/video synchronous communication among the learners.

LTSA collaborative/asynchronous stakeholder's perspective emphasis is on the development, format, protocol and delivery of multimedia within WebCT. This has been achieved as follows:

– Development: The RealNetworks family allows users to bundle several media clips, synchronize them in time and space using the SMIL XML(W3) based language. It specifies the bit rate, and the RealMedia clip information such as author, description, and keywords. However, these media clips, and their corresponding information are not searchable.

– Format: The multimedia clips developed using RealNetworks have a proprietary codec: RealAudio and RealVideo.
– Protocol and delivery: The RTSP (Real Time Streaming Protocols) is used to control the delivery of data with real time properties. The RTSP data packet format used is the RTP delivered over the UDP. The RTSP control connection is the TCP to send instruction and command such as rewind, fast forward, pause and resume.

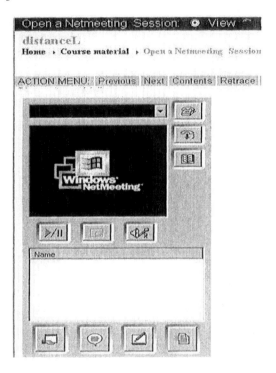

Figure 10-1. Netmeeting integrated in WebCT

Moreover, this stakeholder perspective emphasizes also the collaboration in the Learner entity. WebCT provides several low bandwidth Synchronous/Asynchronous communication tools such as discussion, whiteboard, mail, and chat. In addition, the integration of Microsoft Netmeeting in WebCT (Figure 10-1) provides audio/video/sharing of application among the learners.

Reusability of learner data is possible using API provided by WebCT. It allows the direct access and manipulation of the two separate databases via a command or web-based interface. These databases are the global database and student database. They have built-in fields that cannot be renamed or deleted and other fields that can be added. The global database contains a listing of all users in the WebCT server. A WebCT ID, password, first name, last name, courses, and registered courses describe each user. Moreover, the user data can be imported to the global database in a text file format, and exported in an Excel format. The global database could comply with a standard learner profiles in order to enhance the reusability. The student database is a collection of databases that are specific to each course. This database contains the User ID, password, first name, and last name. For every course, the User ID (in student database) is usually linked to the WebCT ID (in global database).

The reusability between WebCT's platforms at the course level is possible by backup/restore or using the course as a template for other courses with the course structure defined depending on the designer preference. Moreover, there is no easy reuse of modules, lessons, and multimedia presentations from within the same platform, since the library concept is not supported in WebCT and modules must be duplicated in each course. To overcome this problem, a Meta file or a pointer was used to link to these modules stored outside the platform. In addition, The WebCT COBALT will overcome these problems, provide a course and section hierarchy to improve the content sharing. The reusability of WebCT courses in any IMS compliant e-learning system is possible using the IMS Extensible Markup language (XML) importer/exporter utility. This utility allows us to recreate the course structure with the corresponding course content.

5.   CONCLUSION

In this paper, we have presented a new WBT/E that it appears to overcome the reusability and interoperability problems at the learner and course level. It is mainly based on the LTSA, includes the Enhance Model concept that provides the necessary details to the LTSA components, and adds interoperability and reusability at the course and content level. Moreover, this model leads to a reduced course production cost, larger potential market, and life long learning improvement. To illustrate this model, a scenario of collaborative learning stakeholder's perspective was presented. In this scenario, WebCT was used as the distance-learning platform, RealNetworks family for manipulating synchronized multimedia courses integrated in WebCT, and Microsoft NetMeeting for providing audio/video/sharing of application among the collaborators.

REFERENCES

Abdallah R., Benzekeri A., El Hajj A. and Moukarzel I. (2001). Integration of multimedias files in WebCT for the distance learning. *1er Colloque International sur les defies de l'enseignement à distance*, University Antonine- in collaboration with Agence universitaire de la francophonie, Lebanon.

Abdallah R., Benzekeri A., El Hajj A. and Moukarzel I. (2002a). On the Integration of Synchronous Tools in Asynchronous Learning Networks. *International Conference on Research Trends in Science and Technology RSTL2002*, Lebanese American University, Lebanon.

Abdallah R., Benzekeri A., El Hajj A. and Moukarzel I. (2002b). On the use of e-learning standard in a WBT/E model. *In the IFIP International Working Conference Working Group 3.5- Informatics and Elementary Education.-'Learning with technologies in School, home and Community' - Conference Proceedings.* G. Marshall, Y.Katz (ed.) Manchester,UK,July. pp.1-5.

Abdallah R., El Hajj A.,Benzekeri A. and Moukarzel I. (2002c). On the improvement of Course Interoperability in E-learning models. *In the ICEE International Conference on Engineering Education. Conference proceeding*, Manchester UK, August. CD-ROM article index 0024.

Babu S. (2001). *E-learning standards.* [www.cdacindia.com/html/pdf/Session6.1.pdf] 14.6.2002

Benzekri A., Aoun A. and Gert M. (2000). Integrating Web-Based Training into Concurrent Engineering. *In the ICE International Conference on Engineering Education. Conference proceeding*, ICE2000. IRIT, Toulouse ,France

Enhance (2002). Enhanced Aeronautical Concurrent Engineering. [http://www.enhanceproject.com] 14.6.2002

Harvi S.(2000). *Achieving interoperability in E-learning.* [http://www.learningcircuits.org/mar2000/singh.html] 14.6.2002

IEEE (2002). IEEE LTSC Institute of Electrical and Electronics Engineers, Learning Technology Standards Committee [http://ltsc.ieee.org] 14.6.2002

IMS (2002). *IMS Question & Test Interoperability Specifications* [http://www.imsproject.org] 03.09.2002

ISO (2002). International Organization for Standardization - International Electrotechnical Committee, Joint Technical Committee 1, Subcommittee 36 — Information Technology for Learning, Education, and Training (ISO-IEC JTC1 SC36) [http://jtc1sc36.org] 14.6.2002

Microsoft (2002). [http://www.microsoft.com] 14.6.2002

MPEG-4 (2002). *Overview of the MPEG-4 Standard,* [http://mpeg.telecomitalialab.com/standards/mpeg-4/mpeg-4.htm]. 03.09.02

MPEG-7 (2002). *Overview of the MPEG-7 Standard (version 6.0),* [http://mpeg.telecomitalialab.com/standards/mpeg-7/mpeg-7.htm] 03.09.02

RealNetworks (2002). [http://www.RealNetworks.com] 14.6.2002

Robson R. (2000). *Report on learning Technology Standards.* [http://eduworks.com/robby/papers/edmedia2000.pdf] 14.6.2002

WebCT (2002). [http://www.Webct.com] 14.6.2002

W3 (2002). [http://www.w3.org/AudioVideo/] 14.6.2002

11

COLLABORATIVE WORK TOOLS IN LEARNING ENVIRONMENTS
Application in the University of Las Palmas

Mario Marrero[1], Celso Perdomo[1], Jorge Rodríguez[2] and Antonio González[2]
[1] Cabildo de Gran Canaria, C/ Tomás Morales, 35002, Las Palmas GC, Spain
[2] University of Las Palmas de Gran Canaria, Edificio de Ciencias Básicas, Campus Universitario de Tafira, 35017, Las Palmas GC. Spain

Abstract: In this paper, we present HTC, an Internet package for collaborative work. This package is a collaborative and distributed application, which allows users to create their own individual workspaces, which, can in turn, be shared partially or totally with other HTC users. HTC fulfils the following basic objectives: intuitive and easy to use, easy to incorporate into an organization, and allows for global access to resources. Additionally, we present the tool's integration process into the University of Las Palmas de Gran Canaria. From this integration process and the statistical results, we obtain some conclusions. HTC is in its evaluation phase in various Spanish-speaking universities and companies.

Key words: CSCW (Computer Supported Cooperative Work), CSCL (Computer Supported Collaborative Learning, Groupware)

1.   INTRODUCTION

With the implementation of information technologies in organizations, research in the cognitive field was initially focused on the study of the interaction between a human and a machine. In other words, the relationship that exists between an individual user and a computer system for the completion of a task.

This initial approach omits the collaborative aspect that many tasks have. Work is a social phenomenon. There exist thousands of connections and relationships among all of the parties involved in any production process. In general, the most interesting part of any task that provides the highest productivity is that groups work to achieve one common objective. Some statistics show that office workers spend between 30% and 70% of their time in meetings (Cole 1995). For example, in any company there are groups of people dedicated to corporate planning, budgeting, production, sales and other tasks. Nonetheless, many of the most extensive software applications available on the market at this time tend to ignore this fact, providing only for individual work environments.

Collaborative work is necessary due to the following factors: a) Problems are more and more complex, b) Problems are bigger, c) Problems are more and more specialized and d) The solutions to these problems require different aptitudes or abilities.

As a consequence, this brings about a change in attitude, since a) people need to work as members of a team (collaboration); b) people need to exchange information frequently and c) the success of the task not only depends on the merits of each individual worker, but also on the level of cooperation. On the other hand, it implies an organizational change due to the organization's own dynamic bringing about new forms (for permanent adaptation).

On the other hand, it is true that as collaborative work becomes more and more a part of an organization, all of the information that is generated can be filtered, analysed and organized generating knowledge.

In reality, the challenge for many organizations (Dix 1996) consists of being able to use tools such as HTC to eventually know what the organization already knows and have this information be accessible by any team member (with the appropriate permission rights) and from any location within the organization. With HTC, any organization can begin to develop a collaborative project and manage information starting with the following three fundamental objectives:

– Constantly learn how to improve and increase output from meetings and work groups within the organization.
– Interrelate the various work groups and the information they generate.
– Consolidate information to reach a higher level of learning.

The University of Las Palmas de Gran Canaria (UPLGC) has opted to answer these questions generating a system of layers, starting with the physical infrastructure, passing through the Online Information Service UPLGC, the work in groups and finishing off with information management.

This work is presented in five sections. In section 2, we discuss groupware technologies and the basic concepts known as 3Cs. In section 3, we introduce the collaborative work tool design and some aspects of utilization. Followed by the integration process of the tool in the University of Las Palmas de Gran Canaria, and finally, we present some conclusions and future work.

2. GROUPWARE TECHNOLOGIES (WORK IN GROUPS)

We can define a collaborative application as one that helps in the coordination of members of a group with the objective to achieve a common task. In general, this is a distributed application, such that, each participating member of the group works from his/her own workstation, sharing information with the rest of the members of the group.

Additionally, groupware is defined as a technology that allows groups of people to work in teams. The main objective of these technologies is to improve the productivity of work groups. Groupware is supported by three basic pillars - the 3Cs (Becker and Zanella 1998):

1. *Communication.* The members of a work group need to communicate with each other to exchange information.
2. *Collaboration.* Members of the group collaborate contributing, submitting feedback, combining opinions and generating documentation together through the exchange of information.
3. *Coordination.* Groupware technologies allow for the coordination of different members of a group in order to carry out a particular project in common.

3. HTC UTILIZATION

HTC is a collaborative and distributed application where you can create an individual workspace for each user, which can in turn, be shared partially or totally with other HTC users. Sharing workspace area is made possible by establishing collaborative relationships among HTC users.

Below is a list of fundamental requirements needed of HTC within an organization:

- *Ease of use.* The tool should be easy to use by any person with limited knowledge of information technology.
- *Global access.* The tool should do away with spatial barriers that may exist between various members of a workgroup.
- *Easy to incorporate into an organization.* The integration of HTC into any organization should not involve traumatic software migrations to the new system.

- *Access to centralized resources.* Easily create a repository of information resources available in the tool.
  The tool for collaborative work, HTC, offers the following functionality:
- Structure based on objects. HTC simplifies its internal structure into three fundamental objects: folders, files, and notes. Based on these three main objects you can create more complex objects such as discussion forums or work flow systems.
- Internal events component. The basic events defined in HTC are: reading an object, modifying an object, and writing to an object.
- Security component. Authentication by means of a *username* and *password* (or optionally the incoming IP address). Access rights on folders.
- Distinct work areas. Users access their personal workspace when entering the HTC tool. All folders, files, and notes in this workspace belong to the user, and by default, cannot be accessed by any other user. To share any of these objects with another member, the user will need to create a Shared Workspace. This is accomplished by creating a folder, and assigning read/write permissions to the users who will access the shared folder, and will form part of a workgroup.
- Discussion and debate forums component. This is possible as a result of the implementation of the notes object.
- Auditing and Sorting component.
- Work with 124 different file formats. Among the most common files are Word (doc), Adobe Acrobat (pdf), and Powerpoint (ppt). Potentially upload and download files quickly. Recyclable wastebasket.
- Address book. Contains contact information of other HTC users who will participate in your projects.
- Invite other colleagues to participate in a workgroup.
- Create accounts instantly. Without e-mails, without delays, without waiting to receive a confirmation or depending on technical staff to create the account for you.
- Intuitive and easy-to-use web interface.
- Administrator component. Access databases containing registered user information, auditing information, suggestions (based on design or content), internal access statistics, etc.

3.1   Connecting to HTC and registering

HTC is an Internet-based tool which can only be accessed if a user has an Internet connection and browser (IE or Netscape). The URL of the HTC tool is http://www.ulpgc.es/htc. The home page is shown in Figure 11-1.

In this figure, you will find a "New user" icon. Click on it to access the registration form. Choose a username and password with which you will authenticate your identity in HTC. Completing the form automatically creates an account for you or a colleague quickly, easily and immediately.

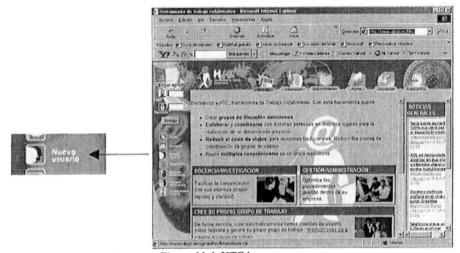

Figure 11-1. HTC home page.

Once the account has been created, access your personal workspace by entering your user name and password into the textbox located on the upper left-hand corner of the home page (Figure 11-1).

3.2 The personal workspace

In your private workspace, you can organize all of your information in folders, files and notes. HTC allows you to share all or part of your personal work area with other HTC members.

The workspace is divided into 2 different areas: chief icons and the work area. The chief icons are arranged according to the three types of basic objects, which are part of the HTC tool:

– *Folders.* Allow you to organize projects and workgroups which you are involved in.
– *Files.* Any type of file in any format which contains information (Word documents, Reports, Articles, Images, Sound files, Video files, etc.).
– *Notes.* Information stored as plain text containing feedback: opinions, comments, objections, etc. Create discussion forums with the notes object.

There are six chief icons: *New, Edit, Delete, Cut, Copy* and *Paste.* Figure 11-2 shows the tool's chief icons.

Figure 11-2. Tool bar with chief icons for each type of object: folders, files, and notes.

3.3   Creating folders

Folders are objects that allow you to organize documents, discussion or debate forums, etc., based on the arrangement you choose for your workspace. For example, you could have a folder for each project you work on, or a folder for each file format you are using, etc.

For example, imagine you want to create a folder where you store the job proposals for the students in your class. Click on the new icon in the Folders section, type the name of the folder "Job Proposals", and click on the Submit button. With these simple steps, you created a new folder similar to what is shown in Figure 11-3.

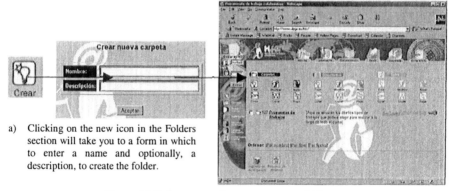

a)   Clicking on the new icon in the Folders section will take you to a form in which to enter a name and optionally, a description, to create the folder.

Figure 11-3. Sequence of steps to create a folder.

Additionally, you can modify the folder properties, cut or copy the folder to later paste in another location of our workspace.

3.4   Creating files

Files are archives in any format. These can range from documents written in Word, presentations developed in PowerPoint, databases, spreadsheets, images, MP3 sound files, videos, etc.

To create a file, click on the new icon in the Files section. In the file creation form, insert the name of the new file, a description (optional), browse to your hard drive for the file to upload to HTC, and choose the appropriate file extension (doc for Word documents, ppt for PowerPoint presentations, etc.).

3.5   Creating notes

Notes are plain text messages that allow you to communicate information quickly, and also establish discussion forums in HTC with other members. Creating notes is much easier than creating files (as specified in the previous section). Clicking on the new icon will take you to a form where you will write the text you want to include in the note.

3.6   Address book

In HTC, you can have an address book with your contacts: people with whom you collaborate on projects, clients, etc.

To add a new contact to your address book, click on the Address Book icon and add a new member. You should know the user name of the person you want to add to your address book, and of course, this person should have an open account at HTC.

3.7   Sharing the workspace

As mentioned earlier, members of HTC create their own accounts and access their own personal workspaces. In this workspace the users can organize and include as many documents as they want, keeping in mind that only they can see them.

If you want to share all or part of the information in your workspace with one or more users, then you will need to create a shared folder. The procedure to share a folder, and any information you store in it, is simple and easily accomplished following three easy steps defined in the online manual.

4. HTC APPLICATION IN A UNIVERSITY ENVIRONMENT. A CASE STUDY: ULPGC

The ULPGC has at its disposal the Online Information Service (OIS) that fulfils two fundamental objectives: to be an open window to society and become a powerful nervous system for internal management.

The working philosophy that identifies OIS is based on the flow of information circulating directly from its origin towards its final destination on the Server, independent of the knowledge people that generate the information have of information technology.

To achieve this objective, on one hand, we have defined and created simple to use tools for any person foreign to the field of information technology, and on the other hand, the directors of the university have promoted and impelled the utilization of these tools among the university community.

In figure 11-4 we define the layers for the distinct technologies in the university. The *hardware* (HW) layer provides the physical resources, which permit the servers to function correctly (networks, mirrored systems, Unix technology, fault redundancy systems, etc.)

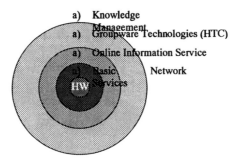

Figure 11-4. Structure of ULPGC's Information Service layers.

The layer, basic network service, provides the logical media, mainly, the communication protocols at the application level (http, dns, dhcp, etc.) Once the Online Information Service layer has been created, the university must approach the level of information management. To reach this goal, it becomes necessary to develop a culture on collaborative work within the community, where information is not published from just one location (or only one author), but that the information is a product of a group of people working together. Therefore, we add to the Online Information Service layer, 2 other layers: groupware and information management.

The publication system in the groupware layer is based on different people working together to create one single document.

In its initial implementation phase, the HTC tool is being used in the University of Las Palmas de Gran Canaria to support and complement teachers and students in their interaction in some courses, among other uses. Thanks to HTC, professors can place didactic information (transparencies, previous exams, notes, etc.) at the student's disposal for a particular subject.

For these work groups in HTC we propose the following folder structure: *Faculty, Academic Calendar, Course syllabus, Academic project, Academic resources, Grades, Bulletin boards* and *Suggestions box.*

The tool is being used in courses such as Biomechanics Movement (Physical Education Department), Geodynamics (department of Marine Sciences), etc. After a month and a half, there are over 1877 registered users. The growth is exponential. At the time of writing, there are over 2441 documents, 1062 folders and 588 distributed notes available to the users.

5. CONCLUSIONS AND FUTURE WORK

From the utilization of the tool, we obtain the following conclusions:
– The group of students that use HTC use it as a repository for personal documents in their own private workspace. In this workspace, they place reports, course notes, experiments, programs, etc. They can access all of these resources independent of where they are, in a science lab or a computer lab, in their home or even in a cyber cafe.
– Professors use HTC as an additional channel through which they distribute additional documentation to the students. The confidentiality of the communication and interaction with the student is maintained since the students themselves define the model of collaboration and sharing of information.
– Debate forums are carried out with questions from the students. The answers are always visible to the students within this area. Course students can read every student's questions and answers. In this way we start to create an FAQ (Frequently Asked Questions) that can be used in future courses. Another advantage to this type of interaction is the anonymity where the user's fear to ask questions disappears.
– Each faculty member uses the HTC tool at their own rhythm. Given the intuitiveness of its usage, faculty staff generate new possibilities for its proper usage and incorporate them into their classes.

Future work includes in the first stage, to obtain experience in the management environment both in universities as well as other institutions

(Cabildo de Gran Canaria and Cabildo de Fuerteventura, among others) since we suspect that the tool can reach its maximum potential in this field. Subsequently, based on this experience proceed with improving certain technical aspects, among them, the definition of a distributed architecture to support a higher number of users and the integration of mobile services for communication and administration. In addition, we are working in offering this package under GNU General Public License, to share it with other universities and educational institutions.

REFERENCES

Becker, K and Zanella A. L. (1998). *A Cooperation Model for Teaching/Learning Modeling Disciplines.* Instituto de Informática. Pontifícia Universidade Católica do Rio Grande do Sul. Porto Alegre. Brazil.

Cole P. (1995). *The Impact of Group Context on Patterns of Groupware Use: A Study of Computer Conferencing as a Medium of Work Group Communication and Coordination.* Center for Coordination Science. MIT (Massachusetts Institute of Technology).

Dix, A. (1996). *Challenges and Perspectives for Cooperative Work on the Web.* HCI Research Centre, School of Computing and Mathematics. The University of Huddersfield. UK.

SECTION 4

ICT TRAINING FOR EDUCATIONAL PROFESSIONALS

12

MANAGING ICT ACCESS AND TRAINING FOR EDUCATORS
A Case Study

Christopher O'Mahony
Information Systems Manager - The Royal High School, BATH, UK

Abstract: This paper reports on a study investigating the use of ICT (Information and Communication Technology) by academic and non-academic staff at an independent English secondary school. Three key areas were investigated: access to ICT inside and outside the school, the perceived and desired ICT ability of staff, and issues preventing increased use of ICT in teaching, learning and administration. Results showed that a major challenge facing the school was not access to ICT resources, but the provision of relevant supportive training for staff.

Key words: School information systems, professional development, educational management, information and communication technology

1.   INTRODUCTION

As secondary schools across Britain get more serious about ICT strategic planning, it is important to build in regular evaluation points to assess the efficacy of ICT investments and management structures (Baker 1995, O'Mahony et al. 1996). In addition to providing a basic level of ICT hardware and software, many schools recognise the importance of staff ICT training. Ability must go hand-in-hand with access, thus leading to confident use of resources for teaching, learning and administration. At the same time, schools are continually challenged to respond to technological change - realising the potential of e-learning innovations.

Research concerning ICT professional development for teachers already exists (Mumtaz 2000), and many exemplary initiatives have been attempted around the world, such as the TILT programme in Australia, and the NOF scheme in the UK (Selwood et al. 2000). Broad-brush initiatives such as these are a useful starting point, but it is noted that staff ICT training must be customised to the needs of individual schools, and individual staff (McDougall & Squires 1997).

This paper presents the results of a survey conducted in September 2001 at an independent girls day and boarding school in the West of England (School X). The survey sought to investigate three things: staff levels of access to ICT both at home and at work; staff levels of use of ICT both at home and at work; and staff perceptions of ability with a variety of ICT applications. Drawing on the work of previous research (McDougall & Squires 1997; Cox et al. 1999; Mumtaz 2000; O'Mahony 2000), research questions were formulated as follows:

– What are the current levels of access to ICT resources among school staff and students?
– What are the current levels of ability with ICT among school staff?
– What are the current levels of use of ICT resources among school staff?

Results indicate that although access to ICT resources is high, staff at School X can improve their integration of ICT use in teaching, learning and administration. High levels of access to ICT resources are reported, well above national averages indicated by Watson et al. (1998). At the same time, despite concentrated pockets of ICT use, the majority of staff use these resources infrequently. The level of ICT training is perceived as low, with the main criticism being a lack of time available for training.

A key element of this study is a reliance on action research methodologies (Hult & Lennung 1980). To this end, conclusions of the paper include practical recommendations for training programmes, home-school network links and carefully targeted ICT resourcing. Although much has been invested, the challenge now is to reap the return on the investment.

2.   BACKGROUND

School X is a member of a Trust of independent girls schools (the XYZ Trust). In 1995, the XYZ Trust made a significant commitment to ICT in its schools. At that time, it embarked on a policy which included a strong investment in ICT infrastructure, including LANs in each school and a Wide Area Network connecting all Trust sites, investments in software and hardware, staff training and ICT management mechanisms. A rollout of ISDN connections was completed in 1997, providing data communications links between schools and Trust Office, as well as access to Trust-wide email services and to the Internet. Local Area Networks in individual schools progressed simultaneously, funded centrally. To make effective use of this infrastructure, the Trust set aside funding on a per capita basis for each school, designed to cover purchasing of PCs and other peripherals, software licenses, consumables, staff training and ongoing maintenance.

An important element of the Trust's initiative was the establishment of IS management posts in each school. Historically, like many other schools, the Trust had relied on enthusiastic teaching staff to provide technical ICT support. As time passed and ICT became more complex and more pervasive, the Trust recognised the need for full-time technical support. By 1998, all Trust schools had either an Information Systems Manager or Network Manager and at least one ICT technician.

School X, as a member of the XYZ Trust, has been a beneficiary of the ICT initiative. Between 1995 and 2001, the number of PCs at the school rose from 40 to 200, connected by a single NT network. All staff and students have personal email addresses provided by the school, the school's administrative information systems have been streamlined, and ICT is in evidence in almost all teaching and learning (School X 2001).

In November 2000, the school was the subject of an Independent Schools Inspection. Despite praising the school in many areas, the inspectors commented that ICT could be better used throughout the school (ISI 2000). The issue for inspectors was not so much quantitative metrics on ICT resources in the school, but rather more qualitative measures as to the effectiveness of those resources. In September 2001, members of the school's senior management team engaged in a whole-school consultation for strategic development, of which ICT was a contributing factor. Part of this consultation included surveys of both staff and students regarding ICT use and ability. Interim results from these surveys are the subject of this paper.

3.   METHODOLOGY

Two surveys were administered to the school community at the beginning of the Autumn Term 2001. A Staff Survey was administered on September 5, 2001, during a full staff study day. 96 responses were received, representing 100% of the school's staff population. On October 9, 2001, a Student Survey was administered through form group assemblies. In total, 426 responses were received, representing 71% of the senior school's student population (Year groups 7 to 13). Responses to both surveys were entered into automated spreadsheets for analysis.

The primary focus of the surveys was their practical element. They were designed to provide swift and immediate feedback to the school's senior management team, enabling them to tailor their ICT strategic planning for the forthcoming years. In this sense, the study had a strong Action Research dimension (Baskerville & Wood-Harper 1996; Klein & Myers 1999). The research provided important signposts for the provision of appropriate access to ICT resources in the school, the provision of customised training programmes for staff, and the fine-tuning of limited ICT budgets to areas so identified.

At the same time, despite the pragmatic nature of the study, every attempt was made to retain academic rigour in the study (Benbasat & Zmud 1999; Kock et al. 1997; Lee 1999). Survey questions were drawn from a bank of questions already used in previous studies by National Statistics (2000), BECTA (2000, 2001a, 2001b) and Research Machines (2000), giving a strong validity to the survey instruments. The use of a survey methodology in itself enables repeatability (Leedy 1993). All survey responses were anonymous and confidential, with no possibility of identifying specific individuals.

Limitations certainly exist. It must be noted that the school's student population is all female, which will have some bearing on the results. Furthermore, consideration should be given to the socio-economic status of both students and staff at the school. The area in which School X is located is generally considered an affluent area, and the school, although offering competitive fees, has a specific position in the local educational market. To this end, it is recommended that a geographically wider study, using the same tools, will give a much more comprehensive answer to the research questions.

4.   RESULTS

Results drawn from the surveys fall naturally into the broad categories proposed in the instruments, and are treated accordingly here as follows:
– Access to ICT at home– questions 1 to 5 – section 4.1
– Access to ICT at work – questions 6 to 9 – section 4.2
– Use of ICT – questions 10 to 15 – section 4.3 and 4.4
– Ability with ICT – questions 16 and 17 – section 4.5
– Difficulties with ICT – question 18 – section 4.6.

4.1   Access to ICT at home

Overall, results drawn from both the staff and student surveys indicated that access to ICT resources was significantly higher than the national average. 92% of staff had access to a computer at home, much higher than the national average of 40% of households (Tables 12-1 and 12-2). 77% of staff had access to the internet from home, as compared with a national average of 38%. For students, the equivalent survey results showed that 91% of students had access to a computer at home, and 85% had access to the Internet from home.

Table 12-1. Home access to computers (Sources: National Statistics 2000, National Grid for Learning 2001)

	% Staff	% Students	Impact2 Average	National Average
Senior School	91%	91%	n/a	
Junior School	95%	n/a	n/a	
TOTAL	92%	91%	n/a	40%

Table 12-2. Home access to the Internet (Sources: National Statistics 2000, National Grid for Learning 2001)

	% Staff	% Students	Impact2 Average	National Average
Senior School	78%	85%	64%	
Junior School	75%	n/a	48%	
TOTAL	77%	85%		38%

In commenting on this surprisingly high penetration of ICT into the homes of school staff and students, closer inspection of the demographics is recommended. It is worth noting that, since 1997, the XYZ Trust has been promoting the use of interest-free loans for personal computer purchases by staff. A good number of staff had taken up this offer, which has clearly helped to raise the proportion of home ICT equipment among staff. Another hypothesis is that a significant number of staff were themselves members of families with school-age children, thus suggesting additional incentives for purchasing ICT equipment for home use.

Research conducted during the Impact2 study (National Grid for Learning 2001) suggests a strong correlation between staff access to ICT at home and staff confidence and competence with ICT. Given the high proportion of both staff and students with access to computers at home, it is interesting to consider the responses to questions regarding actual use of these resources. Analysis of this response is presented in section 4.3.

4.2 Access to ICT at work

In comparison to home access to ICT, it is worth considering access to ICT provided within the school walls (Table 12-3). As already noted in the introduction to this paper, the XYZ Trust has been investing heavily in ICT since around 1995. As a result, it now boasts an enviable student-to-computer ratio across all its schools. At School X, this stood at 1:6 in 2001, significantly higher than the most recently published national averages (Table 12-4). Staff access to computers at school was also high, with a staff-to-computer ratio of 1:2 in 2001. Other key indicators include the amount of expenditure per capita on ICT (Table 12-5), and the number of individual email addresses provided by the school (Table 12-6).

Table 12-3. School Access to ICT

School Access to:	All Staff	Senior	Junior
PC	84.38%	83%	95%
Email	93.80%	96%	95%
Internet	95.83%	92%	95%

Table 12-4. Computer-to-Student Ratios

Ratios	1999	2000	2001
School X	7.0	6.5	6.0
National Average	8.4	7.9	n/a

Table 12-5. ICT Expenditure per Capita (1999-2001)

	1999	2000	2001
School X	£77	£77	£130
National Average	£45	£47	n/a

Table 12-6. Access to Email

	Teachers	Students
School X	100%	100%
Impact2 Average	n/a	67%
National Average	52%	26%

4.3 Use of ICT at home

On average, staff used a home computer for 4 hours per week for school-based tasks, and a further 2 hours per week for non-school based tasks. Staff used their home Internet account for about 1hr 45 minutes each week – 1 hour for personal use and 45 minutes for school tasks. A distinct difference was noted between home ICT use by junior school staff as opposed to their senior school counterparts (Table 12-7).

Table 12-7. Home use of ICT (hours per week) - All Staff

	For Work			Not for Work		
	Junior School	Senior School	Combined	Junior School	Senior School	Combined
Using the Computer	2.63	4.19	3.86	1.13	2.12	1.91
Using the internet	0.78	0.69	0.71	0.93	1.04	1.01
Using email	0.40	0.75	1.01	0.85	1.11	1.05

4.4   Use of ICT at work

On average, staff used a work computer for 7.65 hours per week on school-based tasks. About one hour each week was spent using the Internet at work (Table 12-8).

Table 12-8. Work use of ICT (hours per week) - All Staff

	For Work			Not for Work		
	Junior School	Senior School	Combined	Junior School	Senior School	Combined
Using the Computer	2.00	7.65	6.51	0.05	0.10	0.09
Using the internet	0.55	1.24	0.90	0.00	0.08	0.06
Using email	1.22	0.08	1.10	0.11	0.13	0.13

When responses from administrative staff were eliminated, however, the results for teaching staff were markedly reduced (Table 12-9). The large difference in average ICT work use between academic and administrative staff demanded closer investigation. For academic respondents, 90% claimed to use ICT for less than 10 hours per week – 75% reported less than 5 hours per week. This result begged the question – if access to resources was so high, why was use so low? Part of the answer to this question lay in the responses to subsequent components of the questionnaire.

Table 12-9. Work use of ICT (hours per week) - Administrative vs. Academic staff

	For Work		Not for Work	
	Admin	Academic	Admin	Academic
Using the Computer	20.4	4.86	0.10	0.09
Using the internet	0.1	1.22	0.00	0.07
Using email	4.2	1.75	0.03	0.14

4.5   Ability

The second half of the staff questionnaire considered ICT ability among staff. Question 16 asked staff to rate their current perceived ability with a range of ICT hardware and software. On each of ten items, staff were asked to self-assess their ability in the range 0-3, where 0 signified no ability, and 3 signified expert ability.

A wide range of ability was perceived across departments. Of key concern to the school was any department with an "average" score of less than 0.70. Although perceived ability with items such as email and Word was relatively high, other items that have a growing relevance to teaching and learning were relatively weak. By sorting the data in this way, the school was able to consider training solutions that targeted specific departments, rather than more broad-brush approaches. Using this ranking, it was interesting to note that ICT ability was broadly spread across subject-types. That is, contrary to conventional wisdom, it was not necessarily the 'soft' humanities subjects claiming low ICT ability, and not necessarily the 'hard' numerate subjects claiming high ICT ability. This would indicate that results were driven more by personalities involved, rather than subject stereotypes.

Question 17 asked staff to nominate their desired ability with the same range of items. We took the difference between perceived current ability and desired future ability for each respondent, (that is, Q16 response versus Q17 response) and summed this difference for each application. Results suggested that the school's top training priorities were as follows (Table 12-10). It was pleasing to note that topics classified as more 'basic', such as email, word processing and web searching, came at the bottom of the list. This indicated that staff were generally comfortable with these basic applications, but were also keen to move ahead.

Table 12-10. Training priorities

Application	Priority
Powerpoint	1
Data Projectors	2
Web Design	3
Microsoft Publisher	4
Digital Whiteboards	5
Microsoft Access	6
Microsoft Excel	7
Web Searching	8
Microsoft Word	9
Email	10

The top five training priorities all had a strong focus on teaching and learning, being directly applicable to classroom practice. Their position in the list indicates a desire to incorporate more sophisticated use of ICT into lessons.

It should be noted that since 1996, the school had attempted a number of ICT training initiatives. These ranged from informal self-help style sessions for small groups, through to formal structured training programmes away from the school premises. Such initiatives had varying success, but clearly the baseline for staff ICT ability was gradually improving. Further discussion of staff ICT ability and appropriate training models is given in Section 5.3.

4.6 Perceived difficulties

Respondents were asked to rank ten common issues in terms of their importance to them – "What's holding you back in your use of ICT in the school?" Responses to this question were occasionally incomplete, but sufficient data was collected to give confidence in the analysis. Not surprisingly, the results are in sympathy with other research in this area (Mumtaz 2000). Across the school, the top concerns were as follows (Table 12-11).

Table 12-11. Staff ICT Concerns

Concern	Rank
Time	1
Quantity of classroom ICT resources	2
Quantity of ICT training	3
Quality of classroom ICT resources	4
Quantity of staff ICT resources	5

5. DISCUSSION

It is clear from the survey results and from supporting evidence that the school has made some positive moves with ICT. Expenditure on ICT resources has been significant, continuous and carefully targeted. This has given both staff and students a high level of access to ICT, matched by high levels of access in the home.

At the same time, staff reported relatively low levels of ICT use, both in home and school environments. Staff ICT ability had moved beyond the 'beginner' stage, but staff were expressing difficulty in gaining skills with more sophisticated tools such as presentation graphics, desktop publishing and web publishing. Key issues for staff, preventing the achievement of this objective, included a lack of time, a lack of training, and a lack of ICT resources in the classroom.

5.1 Immediate action

In terms of action research, results from this study provided immediate and practical feedback to the school's ICT strategic planning. For instance, it was clear that a proposed laptop programme was not required, given such a high proportion of computer access at home already. Instead, attention shifted to possibilities for promoting home-school access. Providing access from home to school network resources through a Virtual Private Network appeared to be a necessary and desirable step.

Responding to staff perceived ICT difficulties, school management incorporated many of the outcomes into its wider development planning. Access to staff ICT resources was addressed quickly, with additional high-specification PCs installed in staff areas. The ICT training programme was revisited to target staff's stated priorities, rather than broad-brush introductory skills training. A project was established to re-design the school's intranet, introducing more dynamism and incorporating e-learning principles. To address concerns regarding classroom access to ICT, a project was established to investigate installing a humanities-specific ICT suite for 2002.

One of the more exciting outcomes of the study was the re-launch of the school's ICT Working Party. In order to attract new blood and new enthusiasm, staff nominated for membership were offered one hour's time release per fortnight, to be used for exploring innovative teaching strategies. At the same time, they were offered priority specialised ICT training. It was anticipated that these 'seeds' would then pass on their strategies and new-found skills to colleagues.

5.2   ICT effectiveness model

In synthesising the results drawn from the two questionnaires, it is possible to develop a model for school ICT effectiveness. This model is presented here as a 6-point plan for achieving confident use with ICT. In summary, the 6-point-plan comprises:
- Resources
- Policy
- Departmental commitment
- Training Programme
- Evaluation/appraisal
- Student learning

These six 'pillars' are outlined in the sections following.

5.2.1   ICT resources

A pre-requisite to success with school ICT is the provision of sufficient resources. These resources include network infrastructure, workstation and peripheral hardware, software and human resources. Strong project management must be applied to ensure that the school gains good value for money, at the same time recognising that inferior products do more damage than good. Where possible, hardware and software applications must be well integrated and easy to use (Stevenson 1997).

5.2.2 Curriculum ICT policy (Strategic)

The school must make a clear statement of intent and direction concerning the use of information and communication technologies in curriculum areas. This statement must be visible in school documentation at the senior management level, and be internalised throughout the curriculum. The curriculum ICT policy must articulate well with the school's business and strategic development plans. Specific details of this policy could include a mandated minimum number of hours of ICT use, a target minimum qualification to be attained, or specific ICT-based assessment tasks.

5.2.3 Department commitment (Tactical)

At the Department level, ICT policies must exist which articulate with the wider ICT strategy, and provide necessary detail and context for the respective curriculum area. This policy should express the department's commitment to ICT professional development, and specify expectations of ICT use in the classroom, both in terms of minimum hours and ICT-based tasks.

5.2.4 Teacher professional development

As well as having ICT resources, and having policies regarding the use of ICT in teaching, learning and administration, a robust and measurable professional development programme must be in place. Of course, a teacher's skill with ICT should begin pre-service. This is an area where, in the past, teacher-training institutions have been remiss. As employers, schools have a right to expect training institutions to effectively prepare graduates for the whole classroom experience, which increasingly includes confidence and competence with ICT. One way that this expectation is being made manifest is in job advertisements, which more frequently make explicit reference to ICT skill requirements.

Whatever the pre-existing experiences of staff, an internal professional development programme should, as a starting-point, comprehensively and continuously audit their ICT skill-set. The implementation of an ICT training regime will vary from school to school. Decisions need to be made concerning appropriate venues for training (within school or away from school), timing (within school time or out of school hours) and content (productivity-based or subject-specific). Hiring external trainers has often been the only option for schools but, increasingly, schools are considering the appointment of dedicated training staff within the overall ICT function (O'Mahony 2001).

5.2.5   Staff appraisal and review

The appraisal and review process gives crucial feedback for all aspects of the model. To drive home the message concerning the school's commitment to ICT, effective classroom use of ICT must become a performance indicator for staff. A process must exist whereby the reviewer can flag the reviewee's ICT training needs. This must be communicated to the training function / coordinator, who organises / delivers the required training. Once completed, confirmation of training is passed back along the chain.

As well as providing feedback on staff ability, the appraisal and review process offers the opportunity to flag any issues concerning ICT resourcing or access. These issues, too, must be forwarded to the relevant person / function. Collectively, these items will assist in the formation of subsequent ICT strategies.

5.2.6   Student ICT literacy

The ultimate aim of this model, and in particular the Staff ICT professional development programme, is the improvement of student learning. Thus, complementary to a Staff ICT skills programme is a cross-curricular student ICT skills programme. Transcending the use of ICT in specific subjects, such a programme would provide broad-based exposure to generic ICT skills, including keyboard familiarity, word processing, spreadsheets, presentation graphics, internet searching and 'appropriate ICT use'.

6.   CONCLUSION

The Trust's (and the school's) explicit investment in ICT is demonstrably effective – the ratio of computers-to-students is low, and staff note a satisfying level of access to ICT resources for teaching and learning. At the same time, and generally outside the influence of the school, both staff and students have a high level of access to computers and the Internet from their homes.

In terms of ability, the majority of staff at the school have progressed beyond the 'beginner' stage, and are seeking to broaden and deepen their ICT skills.

Although reporting high access to ICT resources at both home and work, staff note an unremarkable low level of use of these resources. National statistics data shows a general rise in home ICT use across the country, but despite recognition that there is a growing obligation and desire to incorporate ICT elements into teaching and learning, including lesson preparation, teachers report concerns with training and the amount of time available to improve their skills with ICT.

Results from the study are comparable to results reported by other researchers. Like McDougall & Squires (1997) and Visscher & Brandenhorst (2000), it is clear that a well-defined programme for professional development is crucial to success with ICT in the classroom. Like Mumtaz (2000) and Cox et al. (1999), a number of factors exist which inhibit teachers from successful experiences with ICT in the classroom.

Many questions remain. For instance, although staff have a high level of access to ICT at home, a significant minority still do not. 8% of staff do not have a computer at home – 23% do not have access to the Internet at home. How does the school respond to this? How can these staff be encouraged? How should the school best allocate its resources to close this gap? Similarly, with students, 15% still have no home access to the Internet. What implications does this have for home-school ICT access? What implications does this have for their academic progress?

Two key recommendations are made from this study. The first is that the school maintains its commitment to continuous improvement, with and through ICT. The second is that a wider study should be performed, across all XYZ Trust schools in the first instance, to provide a more comprehensive picture of ICT efforts in this unique organisation.

REFERENCES

Baker, B., (1995). The role of feedback in assessing information systems planning effectiveness. *Journal of Strategic Information Systems*. 4, 1, 1995.

Baskerville, R.L., Wood-Harper, T., (1996). A critical perspective on action research as a method for information systems research. *Journal of Information Technology*. 1996, 11, pp235-246.

BECTA (2000). *Connecting Schools, Networking People: ICT planning, purchasing and good practice for the national Grid for Learning.* British Educational Communications and Technology Agency, Coventry.

BECTA (2001a). *Primary Schools of the Future - Achieving today. A report to the DfEE by Becta.* British Educational Communications and Technology Agency, Coventry.

BECTA (2001b). *The Secondary School of the Future. A preliminary report to the DfEE by Becta.* British Educational Communications and Technology Agency, Coventry.

Benbasat, I., & Zmud, R., (1999). Empirical research in Information Systems: the practice of relevance. *MISQ*, Vol 23, No 1, March 1999, pp 3-16.

Cox, M., Preston, C. and Cox, K (1999). *What factors support or prevent teachers from using ICT in their classrooms?* Paper presented at the British Educational Research Association Annual Conference, University of Sussex, Brighton, November 1999.

Hult. M.. & Lennung. S-A.. (1980). Towards a definition of action research: a note and a bibliography. *Journal of Management Studies*, 17, pp241-250.

ISI (2000). *Results of the Inspection of School X.* Independent Schools Inspectorate: UK.

Klein, H.K., & Myers, M.D., (1999). A set of principles for conducting and evaluating interpretive field studies in information systems. *MISQ*, Vol 23, No 1, March 1999, pp 67-93.

Kock, N.F. Jr., McQueen, R.J., Scott, J.L. (1997). Can action research be made more rigorous in a positivist sense? The contribution of an iterative approach. *Journal of Systems and Information Technology*, 1, 1, pp 1-24.

Lee, A.S., (1999). Rigor and relevance in MIS research: beyond the approach of positivism alone. *MISQ*, Vol 23, No 1, March 1999, pp 29-33.

Leedy, P.D. (1993). *Practical Research: planning and design. (5th Ed).* Macmillan, New York.

McDougall, A., and Squires, D., (1997). A framework for reviewing teacher professional development programmes in information technology. *Journal of Information Technology for Teacher Education*, 6, 2, 1997.

Mumtaz, S (2000). Factors affecting teachers use of information and communications technology: a review of the literature. *Journal of Information Technology for Teacher Education*, 9, 3, 2000.

National Grid for Learning (2001). *Impact2: Emerging findings from the evaluation of the impact of information and communications technologies on pupil attainment.* : DfES. Annesley.

National Statistics (2000).

O'Mahony, C.D., Wild, P., Selwood, I.D., Reyes, M.G., Kraidej, L. (1996). Evaluation strategy for ITEM quality. In *Information Technology in Educational Management for the Schools of the Future,* Fung, A.C.W. et al (eds). Chapman & Hall, London.

O'Mahony, C.D., (2000). *The evolution and evaluation of information systems in NSW Secondary schools in the 1990s: the impact of values on information systems.* PhD Thesis (unpublished): Macquarie University, NSW.

O'Mahony, C.D. (2001). *I.S. Management in Schools - evolving towards integration.* Proceedings: UK Academy of Information Systems Annual Conference (UKAIS2001), University of Portsmouth, April 2001.

Research Machines PLC (2000). *The RM G7 (8) Report 2000 comparing ICT provision in Schools.* RMplc, Abingdon.

SCHOOL X (2001). *School X ICT Action Plan 2001-2.* (Unpublished).

Selwood, I.D., Smith, D., & Wisehart, J. (2000). Supporting teachers through the National Grid for Learning. In *Pathways to institutional improvement with information technology in educational management*, Nolan, C.J.P., Fung, A.C.W. & Brown, M.A. (eds). Kluwer, Boston.

Stevenson Committee (1997). *Information and Communications Technology in UK Schools - An Independent Enquiry (The Stevenson Report).* Pearson, London. Or rubble.ultralab.anglia.ac.uk/stevenson/ contents.html

Visscher, A.J. and Brandenhorst, E.M. (2000). How should school managers be trained for managerial school information system usage? In *Pathways to institutional improvement with information technology in educational management*, Nolan, C.J.P., Fung, A.C.W. & Brown, M.A. (eds). Kluwer, Boston.

Watson, D., Blakeley, B., Abbott, C., (1998), Researching the use of communication technologies in teacher education. *Computers and Education*, 30, pp15-22.

13

ASSESSING THE ICT TRAINING CONDITIONS FOR EDUCATIONAL MANAGERS

Javier Osorio
Las Palmas de Gran Canaria University. Department of Management. 35017 Las Palmas de Gran Canaria. Spain

Abstract: Human resources are a critical issue of the Information Technology for Educational Management field (ITEM). Within this issue, computer usage training takes up a key position. In order to identify the potential and, therefore, the utility of a computerized information system the user will previously need to develop some skills to use it, which is possible with an adequate training process. However, experience shows that, very often, training programs are influenced by the environment of the training process. The purpose of this paper is to integrate previous research on training in order to develop a framework which can help identify opportunities and threats owing to environmental factors that can decisively affect a training program's success.

Key words: Training, educational management, environmental analysis, ICT

1.   INTRODUCTION

Managers' effective use of information systems for educational management is a critical factor that can be an indicator of the information system's usefulness. Within this issue, training in computer usage plays a leading role due to the importance of knowing not only how to use the system but also its potential capacity. Therefore, the appropriate design of training courses is vitally important. Visscher and Branderhorst (2001) tried to establish a basis for the effective design of training courses in information systems usage for school managers. They started out with evidence of very little information and communication technology (ICT) support to managerial tasks, although most secondary schools[6] in developed countries use computer-assisted school information systems to operate their organisations. According to these authors, this support is concentrated in the administrative area, thus ignoring the potential contribution to managerial work. There is no doubt that training school managers in computer usage is a very specific study field, so literature on this topic is scarce but exhaustive (see for instance Fung 1995; Selwood 1995 and Fulmer 1996). As stated by Visscher and Branderhorst (2001:148), although there is strong empirical evidence that user training greatly influences the degree of information systems usage, little is known about the ideal contents of courses to train educational managers in this matter. In their research project they tried to identify the characteristics that a training course should have in terms of contents and instructional features to successfully promote the managerial usage of computer supported school information systems.

However, a well-designed course can fail dramatically if other contextual factors are not taken into account. Most of those variables are external to the designer and cannot be controlled, although their negative impact can be foreseen and prevented and, on the other hand, their positive effects can be exploited. If the objective is to design a course that works, then it is also necessary to suit it to the constraints and the environment where it is going to take place. Analysis of environmental factors can offer a preview of the expected probability of success of the course's design and implementation. This success likelihood is directly related to the environment's attractiveness, and so a situation is attractive, that is to say, favourable for the training process, according to the results of analysis of external factors that can be of influence. Therefore, the probability of achieving training goals increases as attractiveness also does. The result of the analysis could be a sort of attractiveness measure associated with a recommended plan of action. Such a plan can lead either to progress in the course design and implementation or to stop and reconsider the situation, trying to discover alternative ways to change the environmental constraints in order to succeed.

The objective of this paper is to contribute to set an analysis framework to evaluate the likelihood of success in the development of training courses for utilization of computerized educational information systems at managerial level. With this aim in mind, the methodology to apply will consist on reviewing literature on contextual factors affecting the training process where variables such as ICT, management, organisational features and managers' profile are present. From the review, a list of factors will

---

[6] The same can be said about primary schools (Selwood et al. 1995; Nolan et al. 1998) and higher education institutions (Bricall, 2000).

arise. Then a systematic method will be proposed to analyse the influence of such factors on the global attractiveness of the training process' environment. Finally, a measure indicating the most feasible plans of action will constitute the final output of the framework.

2. ENVIRONMENTAL FACTORS

There is a wide body of literature dealing with training issues. Having a look at journals focused on different areas of activity (i.e. business, healthcare, education, public sector) and even those focused on specific business functions (i.e. operations management, marketing, human resources) shows that training is a recurrent theme. They usually address precise matters and problems, setting important variables which are key for the success or failure of training programs carried out in the publications' scope. These variables are partly context-specific, but there is also a set of them that are present in almost all study areas, which can be catalogued as general variables. These general variables can be taken as a reference together with some other more specific ones adapted to the environment in which we centre our analysis.

We have identified several sets of variables extracted from different dimensions. All in all, they constitute the factors that may contribute to the success of a course on computer usage for educational managers. The purpose can be graphically described as shown in Figure 13-1. Here we can see that empirical evidence of high usefulness of educational managers' training in computer usage leads directly to consider which should be the contents of this training to ensure a profitable course, undoubtedly an important issue. However, between both dimensions there should also be some mechanism to evaluate contextual factors, those of an environmental nature, which can be decisive to guarantee that a training program can be designed and implemented with a high probability of success.

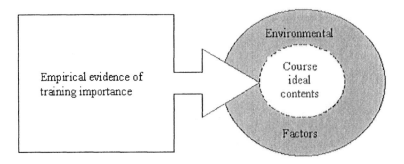

Figure 13-1. Elements of the training process

The analysis framework can be established referring to other authors' work on training topics. From a general perspective, most papers on the subject attempt to establish broad guidelines including general scope variables that experience has proven useful in almost every context. Many of these variables are applicable to any training process and they can be separated into two groups. The first one deals with personal motivation and the reasons that can encourage someone to engage in a training program. The second group relates to the availability of resources, that is to say, the means to aid achievement of training goals. Following previous research (Huczynski and Lewis 1980; Noe 1986; Baldwin and Ford 1988; Garavaglia 1993; Seyler et al. 1998; Gonzales et al. 1999), variables that can influence the training process have been included in the next two groups of factors:

Factor 1: Motivation (Perspectives after completing the training program).
– Expectancy of increased wages.
– Career development.
– Social reconnaissance.
– Personal self-esteem.
– Personal self-satisfaction.
– Increased capacity for autonomous decision-making.
   Factor 2: Availability of resources.
– Well-conditioned place.
– Material resources.
– Documentation.
– Easy access to trainer
– Course schedule.

Now we will proceed to identify three dimensions that comprise variables which have been mentioned in apparently disparate fields, but that can be usefully included in the topic dealt with in this paper. The reason lies in the varied nature of educational managers' training, where different matters converge. They are related to:

1. Management work. Managers' specific training must concentrate on acquiring skills regarding unstructured problem analysis, access to sources of information, action planning, resource management and company activities supervision. However, managers' lack of time must not be forgotten, as it will limit their dedication to learning new skills.
2. Social and psychological attitudes related to computer usage. Factors such as prevalent organisational and individual values, the capacity to influence or be influenced by pressure groups, trainee's age and his/her previous training are of major importance. This is true in as much as the first sign of a training program's success or failure relates to trainees' attitude during the process.
3. New technologies training. Information technology, as any new technology, means new opportunities and threats to people who have to incorporate it into their professional activities. It can even block the introductory process unless factors such as job permanence, acceptance of innovation and leadership counteract, balancing the negative effect of aversion to change.

These three perspectives can be combined and reduced to two groups of variables (two factors). These can complement the two factors mentioned above (motivation and availability of resources) in order to make up the proposed framework for the environmental analysis of training conditions. The two latter groups could be established as follows:

Factor 3: Personal Profile.

- Age.
- Academic degree.
- Professional experience.
- Management experience.
- Familiarity with computers.
- Previous computer-related courses.
- Attitude towards new challenges.
- Time availability.

Factor 4: Organisational Culture.

- Acceptance of innovation.
- Free flow of information within the organisation.
- Employees' involvement in redesigning organisational processes.
- Co-operation amongst employees.
- Capacity to take part in training designing.
- Level of knowledge management in the organisation.
- Institutional sponsorship of computer training.

Once these four factors have been identified, as well as the list of variables which in each case might influence the training program's success, it is time to articulate some sort of measure to use as reference in a particular training situation. The objective, as we have already mentioned, is to foresee to some extent the probability of the program's success. The concept of success in this context is a complex one. Nevertheless, we can agree that a training course on computer usage by educational managers may be tagged as 'successful' if, once concluded, the attendant has acquired the necessary skills to interact with the computer and has learnt to effectively apply these skills to improve his/her performance.

Therefore, the objective is to establish a global estimation of training conditions' attractiveness, which can favour or hinder a training process on computer usage for educational managers. This estimation can help identify actions to improve training results. If this estimation advises to proceed with the training process, then the next step would be to design the course contents, a matter that has been comprehensively addressed by Visscher and Branderhorst (2001).

3.   IMPLEMENTATION OF THE ANALYSIS FRAMEWORK

Aiming to obtain an estimation of training's success, a sequence of steps is proposed. In general terms, the mechanism consists of making a succession of weighed averages in which weights will always be contingent on the situation in which the training program is going to take place. The first step would be to carry out a separate analysis of all the factors that influence the process.

Every factor will be analysed making use of the sets of related variables already identified. As not all variables have the same importance in the analysis context, they will be assessed on a scale that ranges from 0 to 10. Justification of this method lies in the fact that some variables are more determinant than others for the courses' success. Thus, we try to avoid excessive simplifications that could erroneously concede all variables equal importance. It also tends to ensure prior examination of these variables by the course designer, who must take the organisation's features into account and decide which variables are truly important. Total values must add 10. This is just to make sure that results between the various factors involved in the analysis process are homogeneous.

Once variables have been pondered, the next step is to establish a value for the attractiveness profile of every variable within a specific factor. A Likert scale will be used, with values ranging from 1 (very low attractiveness) to 5 (very high attractiveness), with 3 as an intermediate and neutral value. This reflects the environment's situation regarding a certain variable and whether it contributes to make the training processes' environment more attractive.

The last step is just a mathematical one, which consists of multiplying weight by profile value for each variable, thus obtaining the weighed attractiveness profile. To this we add all weighed profiles previously calculated. The result of the addition will be an indicator of the degree of attractiveness for that factor. The total attractiveness value consequently ranges between 10 and 50. A value of 10 means that the factor under analysis contributes poorly, negatively indeed, to create a climate or environment which promotes a training program's success. At the opposite end, a value of 50 means a high or positive contribution to obtain an environment suited for a better training. Halfway, a value of 30 implies a neutral position, in which a factor does not affect the environment's attractiveness neither in a positive nor negative way. The next tables show examples of tables to obtain the attractiveness of each factor, starting with personal motivation. They are merely random examples that only intend to describe the analysis tool.

Table 13-1. Example of attractiveness calculation for the 'Personal motivation' factor

PERSONAL MOTIVATION								
Variables	Weight	Attractiveness Profile						Weighed Attractiveness Profile
		V. Low		Neutral		V. High		
		1	2	3	4	5		
Expectancy of increased wages	3.5			√				10.5
Career development	2.5					√		12.5
Social reconnaissance	1.5	√						3
Personal self-esteem	1.0			√				3
Capacity of autonomous decision making	1.5			√				4.5
Total Weights:	10	Total Attractiveness:						33.5

Comments to table 13-1: In this hypothetical case we see that 'Career development' is the best-profile variable (5), even though its weight (2.5) is lower than 'Expectancy of increased wages' (3.5) is. The latter variable's profile, though, is not so good (3). This shows that the prospect of a wage increase is ambiguous, in the sense that following the course does not guarantee an increase but neither does it rule it out completely. On the other hand, there are very good prospects for career development for those who take part in training. This is an important attractiveness and can ensure that course attendants become highly involved with it.

Table 13-2. Example of attractiveness calculation for the 'Availability of resources' factor

AVAILABILITY OF RESOURCES

Variables	Weight	Attractiveness Profile					Weighed Attractiveness Profile
		V. Low		Neutral		V. High	
		1	2	3	4	5	
Well-conditioned place	3				√		12
Material resources	2				√		8
Documentation	1.5		√				3
Easy access to trainer	1			√			3
Time availability	2.5		√				5
Total Weights:	10	Total Attractiveness:					31

Comments to table 13-2: In this hypothetical case we can see that two highly important resources such as a well-conditioned space to carry out training (3) and availability of material resources (2) are conveniently offered by the organisation (attractiveness profile = 4). This is a positive element in making the course more attractive. On the other hand, though, another outstanding variable such as the time availability because of the course's timetable (2.5) is not attractive (2), as it makes attendance difficult for trainees. As this could become a significant drawback some solution should be provided to overcome it, such as reducing working hours during the period covered by the course.

Table 13-3. Example of attractiveness calculation for the 'Personal profile' factor

PERSONAL PROFILE

Variables	Weight	Attractiveness Profile					Weighed Attractiveness Profile
		V. Low		Neutral		V. High	
		1	2	3	4	5	
Age	0.5			√			1.5
Academic degree	1				√		4
Professional experience	1				√		4
Management experience	1			√			3
Familiarity with computers	3		√				6
Previous computer-related courses	2		√				4
Attitude towards new challenges	1.5	√					1.5
Total Weights:	10	Total Attractiveness:					24

Comments to table 13-3: This hypothetical case reflects a common situation regarding computer usage training amongst executives of many organisations. Very often we find people with ample professional experience and high responsibilities within the company but with hardly any previous contact with computers. Highly weighed variables, such as familiarity with computers (3), previous computer-related courses (2) and the attitude towards new challenges (1.5) have a low attractiveness profile (values 2, 2 and 1 respectively). This results in a low total attractiveness rate for the 'Personal profile' factor (24). Therefore, course design must stress that training can be determinant to use computers as a regular work tool. It must also keep in mind attendants' low computer-related skills.

Table 13-4. Example of attractiveness calculation for the 'Organisational culture' factor

ORGANISATIONAL CULTURE

Variables	Weight	Attractiveness Profile					Weighed Attractiveness Profile
		V. Low		Neutral		V. High	
		1	2	3	4	5	
Acceptance of innovation	2					√	10
Free flow of information	2.5				√		10
Employees' involvement in redesigning organisational processes	1				√		4
Co-operation amongst employees	1			√			3
Capacity to take part in the training design	2.5				√		10
Degree of knowledge management in the organisation	1				√		4
Total Weights:	10			Total Attractiveness:			41

Comments to table 13-4: This hypothetical case shows a situation in which employees' concern in company affairs is highly valued, together with a strong tendency towards innovation and the acceptance of new management techniques. The high total attractiveness rate reached for 'Organisational culture' shows that the organisation makes developing training programs easy. The variable that considers the chance of attendants helping to design the course could be fundamental, as it implies a flexible attitude towards their needs, regarding, for example, the course's duration or it's schedule.

Once all four factors that influence a training programs environment have been analysed, the final step is to obtain an overall measure of attractiveness as a result of weighing all factors taken into account. Similarly to previous analysis, every factor has to be weighed using a scale from 0 to 10 according to their importance in the specific context in which the analysis takes place. This is because, once again, not all factors are equally important when designing a course. Each centre's situation and the context in which the program is to be developed imply the need to establish critical factors and how they will affect success likelihood according to their higher or lower attractiveness rate. The total weight must also be 10. Then, the previously calculated attractiveness values for every factor have to be multiplied by this weight to obtain a weighed value of attractiveness for every factor. The addition of these latter values constitutes the final global attractiveness rate. This value ranges from 100 to 500. The higher the value the higher the attractiveness to design and implement a training program is as well and thus the probability of success. A value of 300 represents the middle point. This is an ambiguous situation where it is necessary to carefully analyse the opportunities and threats before going ahead with the training process. A result in the lower interval means that it is more advisable to try to improve the environmental situation or prevent threats than to proceed with the training program. The next table (5) shows an example of this last step of the analysis.

Table 13-5. . Example of global attractiveness calculation

GLOBAL ATTRACTIVENESS

Factors	Weights	Each factor's attractiveness rate (obtained from previous tables)	Weighed factors' attractiveness
Personal motivation	3	33.5	100.5
Resources availability	2	31	62
Personal profile	2	24	48
Organisational culture	3	41	123
		Global	
Total Weights:	10	Attractiveness:	333.5

Comments to table13-5: This table contains results from previous factor's attractiveness analysis. Here the importance assigned to each factor is similar. The greatest threat for the course's success comes from the 'Personal profile' factor (attractiveness 24) and it should be given special attention when designing the course in order to avoid failure. On the other hand, the main chance of success comes from the 'Organisational culture' (attractiveness 41) which distinctly promotes training. 'Personal motivation' (attractiveness 33.5) and 'Availability of resources' (attractiveness 31) are neutral factors, as such values are close to the middle of the scale (30).

The global attractiveness value obtained can be placed on a graphic scale as shown in Figure 13-2, which reflects the success probability of the intended training program. Values to the right of 300 display an attractiveness that is favourable to developing the course. On the other hand, all values to the left of this middle point should be carefully evaluated before going ahead with training.

4.   FINAL THOUGHTS

Obviously this framework has to be tested by means of a longitudinal analysis to demonstrate its usefulness. However, we consider that the idea that a training program's environment can decisively affect its outcome is intuitively valid. No matter how well a course's contents are designed, if the combination of external or environmental variables is not propitious the likelihood of success is severely diminished. This not only leads to considerable waste of effort and resources, but most importantly to psychological inhibition to further training. This is not an affordable cost in such a highly changing scenario as that of computerised educational management.

> Global attractiveness rate (represented by a circle) resulting from previous hypothetical analysis.

Very Low Attract.	Low Attractiveness	Medium Attractiveness	High Attractiveness	Very High Attract.
100	200	300	400	500
It is probably impossible to carry out the training program due to lack of resources or severe problems that prevent it.	The training program should not be put into practice due to a high probability of failure.	Threats to the program's success should be carefully analysed in order to find ways to overcome detected problems. If these cannot be resolved, postponing training is recommended.	Even though likelihood of success is quite high, it is advisable to examine negative factors and try to solve them.	The probability of success is high. The high attractiveness rate of all factors can justify an ambitious training program.

Figure 13-2. Graphic representation of the resulting global attractiveness value

REFERENCES

Baldwin, T. and Ford, J. (1988). Transfer of Training: A Review and Directions for Future Research. *Personnel Psychology,* 41, pp.63-106.

Bricall, J. (2000). *Informe Universidad 2000*. Conferencia de Rectores de Universidades Españolas.

Cranton, P. (1994). Self Directed and Transformative Instructional Development. *Journal of Higher Education,* 65, 6, pp.727-744.

Fulmer, C. (1996). Training School Administrators to use Information Systems: A Review of Research. *International Journal of Educational Research,* 25, 4, pp.351-361.

Fung, A. (1995). "Managing Change in ITEM". In *Information Technology in Educational Management*, B. Barta, M. Telem and Y. Gev, (eds.), Chapman & Hall, London.

Garavaglia, P. (1993). How to Ensure Transfer of Training. *Training and Development Journal,* 47, 10, pp.63-68.

Gonzales, B.; Ellis, Y.; Riffel, P. and Yager, D. (1999).. Training at IBMs Human Resource Service Center: Linking People, Technology and HR Processes. *Human Resource Management,* 38, 2, pp.135-142.

Huczynski, A. and Lewis, J. (1980). An Empirical Study into the Learning Transfer Process in Management Training. *Journal of Management Studies,* 17, pp.227-240.

Noe, R. (1986). Trainees Attributes and Attitudes: Neglected Influence on Training Effectiveness. *Academy of Management Review,* 11, pp.736-749.

Nolan, C.; Fulmer, C. and Taylor, R. (1998).. Four computerized school information systems: summary discussion. In *The integration of information for educational management*. (pp. 169-173), C. Fulmer, B. Barta and P. Nolan, (eds.), Felicity Press, Whitefield, ME.

Selwood, I. (1995). "The Development of ITEM in England and Wales". In *Information Technology in Educational Management*, B. Barta, M. Telem and Y. Gev, (eds.), Chapman & Hall, London.

Selwood, I.; Wild, P. and Millin, D. (1995). Introduction of IT in school management: approaches, preparation, human and political aspects. Discussion held in the 1st ITEM International Conference. In *Information Technology in Educational Management*, B. Barta, M. Telem and Y. Gev, (eds.), Chapman & Hall, London.

Seyler, D.; Holton III, E.; Bates, R.; Burnett, M. and Carvalho, M. (1998). Factors Affecting Motivation to Transfer Training. *International Journal of Training and Development,* 2, 1, pp.2-16.

Visscher, A. and Branderhorst, E. (2001). How should School Managers be Trained for Managerial School Information System Usage? In *Pathways to Institutional Improvement with Information Technology in Educational Management*, P. Nolan, A. Fung and M. Brown, (eds.), Kluwer Academic Publishers. Boston.

14

MANAGING LEARNING ENVIRONMENTS IN SCHOOLS
Developing ICT Capable Teachers

Maureen Lambert and Patrick Nolan
Massey University, Palmerston North, New Zealand

Abstract: The use of information and communication technology (ICT) in New Zealand educational institutions, as in other countries, has proved to be problematic with outcomes falling far short of expectations. This paper addresses the problem by suggesting a more holistic approach to professional development that takes into account the school-learning environment, including school culture, in an effort to develop educational practitioners as 'all-round' capable ICT-using professionals. To this end, this paper presents and discusses a schematic model of ICT functions and use in school systems, organised hierarchically to accommodate complexity and differentiation between automating and informating functions. The basic argument of the paper is that professional development should be linked directly to the contexts where ICT may be used professionally. Further, development will be optimally effective by identifying and addressing two simultaneous pathways namely, learning and teaching, and administration and management, with emphasis provided during transitions between levels of use. Key aspects of development that support effective ICT use include understanding the multi-functional and multi-tasking nature of the technology, vesting locus of control in users and integrating ICT into everyday professional work. Ongoing research is proposed to further test and demonstrate the efficacy and robustness of the model.

Key words: Information and communication technology, professional development, learning environments

1.   INTRODUCTION

In an opening address to Parliament in 2002, the New Zealand Prime Minister, Helen Clark, identified information and communication technology (ICT) as one of the three major areas of development for increasing New Zealand economic performance. While all sectors of society, including the economy, will be expected to address the priorities, the response of the education system will be key. In order for the priority to be actualised it will be necessary for education institutions to raise the ICT skills of all learners, from preschool to tertiary, to sustain the demand for life long learning and to meet economic performance objectives. A prerequisite for this to occur will be that teachers themselves become ICT literate and ultimately capable ICT-using educational professionals. Successive New Zealand governments have targeted development in this area as one of the three top development priorities for education (along with literacy and numeracy), with access to ICT tools and professional development a key means to support developments. In reality professional development for ICT use, especially computerised school information systems, has been ad hoc and episodic compared with the other two areas.

2.   PURPOSE

The purpose of the paper is to present a model for explaining and guiding the professional development of school practitioners as capable and confident ICT-using professionals. The model embodies the findings of research across a range of related areas of use of ICT in education. These include professional development of teachers (McKinnon and Nolan 1989; Education Review Office 2000), the uptake, implementation and use of computerised systems (Nolan, Ayres and McKinnon 1996) and on the role of culture (Stewart 2001). It embodies, equally, contemporary experience of working with New Zealand schools over the past decade that has helped to clarify and make explicit the underlying complexity of the operation of schools, and their various environments and systems that might be better administered and managed with the aid of ICT. The experience, and research (Nolan et al. 2001), highlights specifically the necessity to conceive of professional development in terms of sequences of development as individuals progressively acquire new ICT capabilities and skills necessary to administer and manage a diversity of school functions and activities. In the model, the functions and activities are portrayed as ranging from relatively simple to complex. The ICT systems and tools most appropriate to support them vary similarly in complexity. Thus, professional development strategies and approaches are required which can accommodate both, as the individuals who seek and get professional development grow and develop as accomplished ICT-using professionals.

3.   BACKGROUND

Since formation of the ITEM Working Group 3.7 in 1994, New Zealand research on information technology and educational management has addressed many aspects of this topic. They include virtually all the contents of the Visscher (1996) model of computerised school information systems covering:

– use and levels of use (Nolan 1995; Nolan & Ayres 1996),
– system development and implementation (Nolan, et al. 1996),
– conceptions of a good school information system (Nolan & Ayres 1996),
– emerging conceptions of schooling likely to impact on system
  development and design (Nolan & Lambert 2001) and
– approaches to professional development for the users and potential users
  of computerised school information systems (Nolan, Brown and Graves
  2001).

Of all the aspects, professional development is the most recurrently problematic and the most important if the potential of contemporary ICT systems and tools is to be fully realised in school education. As discussion below elaborates, currently such realisation is far from happening and the gap between access and use of ICT now available to schools is probably, if anything, wider than a decade ago. The area of teacher ICT literacy continues to be problematic, with technology developments increasingly outstripping the ability of the teaching community to exploit its potential.

4.   ICT PATHWAYS – DIVERGENT EVOLUTION

Generally speaking, ICT use and conceptions of its use in New Zealand school education over the past twenty to thirty years have been evolving along two separate pathways. This has occurred simultaneously, though somewhat divergently, and in a chaotic not orderly or planned manner. We refer to the pathways here as the learning and teaching (L & T) and the school administration and management (A & M) pathways. For the most part, they were laid down for different purposes by teachers and learning theorists on the one hand and school administrators and organisational and systems theorists on the other. Each had seemingly different agendas and interests in how and who might best use ICT (or computers in the early days).

The metaphor of the pathway is useful because it suggests a journey that is ongoing with destinations along the way in the form of new developments and ideas about what is possible and what works best, either to promote student learning and development or manage and administer schools better. Recently, two factors that we examine later in the paper, locus of control and accessibility to ICT by an increasingly wider range of users, have influenced the direction of developments and use patterns on both pathways. With learning and teaching, the trend has been towards greater student control of ICT tools for learning and away from teacher control and instructional systems (McKinnon and Nolan 2001). With administration and management, the trend is towards greater participation by teachers supported by computerised information systems, usable in classrooms and across school levels with less emphasis on computer assisted school administration from the school administrative office (Nolan and Lambert 2001). Both trends are occurring in response to new ICT developments. They reflect also a trend toward schools becoming participatory learning communities with a corresponding de-emphasis of the hierarchic organisation aspect of schools. Both trends necessitate not only reconsideration of ways that ICT might be employed for both learning and teaching and school administration and management but also approaches to professional development for teachers and other school personnel in order that they might more readily and effectively access the ICT systems and tools available.

5.   CONVERGENT EVOLUTION

We believe that such reconsideration is timely because in the last decade or so conversations between users, developers and researchers when the L & T and A & M pathways crossed suggest that a convergent evolution is taking place in thinking and developments, replacing the divergent evolution of the past. Two key outcomes have arisen from this. The first is a more holistic conception of how to use ICT in education due to the multi-functionality and connectivity of modern ICT (viz the Internet) which is making ICT much more accessible to and usable by a diversity of users and potential users. The second is individuals (whether teacher, school administrator, student or parent) developing as 'all round' high-level generalist users. In New Zealand schools, school staffs and students alike have access to ICT and Internet connectivity on a par with other countries' school systems. The Government's Information Technology Advisory Group (ITAG 2000) estimates that:

- Internet access is now available in 96% of all 2300 New Zealand primary schools and in 99% of all 340 secondary schools; and that
- In primary schools the computer/student ratio is 1:13 and in secondary schools it is 1:7.

While the data on access indicates a seemingly impressive accomplishment in relation to acquisition of ICT across the whole school system, anecdotal evidence suggests that the actual use and levels of ICT use are far less impressive. Researchers and policy makers (ERO 2000) have expressed concern about the disparity between access and use but their concern is no less than that of teachers. A New Zealand survey (Lai, Pratt, & Trewern 2001) revealed that in the Otago Technology project 86% of teachers and 88% of the ICT coordinators identified ICT as the preferred area for professional development.

6.   ICT ACCESS AND USE

In perhaps the most authoritative international research, Cuban (1999) has shown that teachers vary considerably in the ways they use ICT, from non-users to serious and sophisticated users who utilize of a wide range of applications. Interestingly, he reported that many teachers actively resist even contemplating the use of ICT. In the North American schools of Cuban's research (1999) over 50% of elementary teachers reported themselves to be ICT non-users. Only 1 in 10 said they were "serious users", e.g., they employed such applications as spreadsheets and databases for the analysis and reporting of student performance and their students routinely carried out multimedia class projects. Also, they typically were the only teachers who used ICT for the management and analysis of school information and to support decision-making and the implementation and review of school policy. In secondary schools, 2 out of 10 teachers were identified as serious users of ICT while 40% of teachers were reported to be non-users. While no comparable research evidence is available in New Zealand, we would speculate that the situation here mirrors that in North America.

Observers and commentators commonly have explained the disparity between access and use, as being the outcome of teacher resistance. Cuban (1999) argues, however, that such an explanation is not credible. According to Knezeck et al. (2000), resistance is a state of affairs not an explanation of why teachers will or will not use ICT. They propose *"will, skill and access"* as the three specific conditions necessary to promote teacher uptake and use of ICT with incorporation of it routinely into thinking and practice:

Will is indicated by positive attitudes toward ICT and the desire to explore its possibilities for particular practical purposes and it can account for up to 40% of the variance in explaining ICT uptake.

Skill is indicated by level of confidence and competency to perform specific functions within a particular program and likewise it accounts for 40% of the variance.

Access is indicated by an individual's ability to procure a computer and relevant software for personal use on a regular basis and as needed. This factor accounts for only 10% of the explanation of uptake but remains important in the sense that without access any progress would be denied.

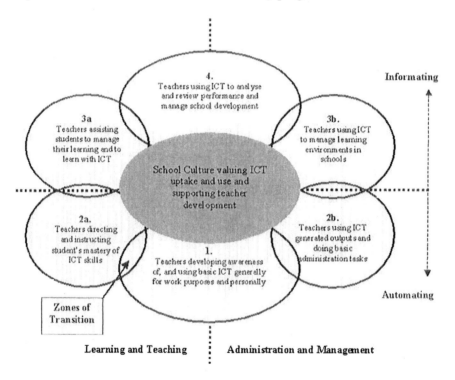

Figure 14-1. A Schematic Model of ICT Functions and Use in School Systems

Professional development in New Zealand has tended to incorporate all three factors but commonly the focus predominantly has been on access at the expense of the development of will and skill. Thus, once the novelty of access has worn off, then in the absence of will and skill the effect of professional development thus conducted tends to wash out in the medium term and ongoing use and development towards more sophisticated use is curtailed. Pockets of professional development around New Zealand that embody the Knezeck et al. (2000) formula have produced more enduring outcomes. We suggest here, however, that the potential of the Knezeck et al. research is best likely to be realised when the factors revealed by it are incorporated into a model which encompasses: (i) the full range of types of uses to which ICT can and might increasingly be put; and (ii) the multiplicity and complexity of functions that constitute the essential work of schools. The model presented here for this purpose is outlined in Figure 14-1.

7. THE ROLE OF SCHOOL CULTURE

Persistently, experience and research (Nolan et al. 2001; Stewart 2001) show that the presence of a 'school culture which value ICT uptake and use and supports teacher development' to be a condition vital for the ongoing implementation, integration and renewal of ICT use in schools across the two broad L&T and A &M domains of ICT use already identified.

In the model, teachers are identified as the key actors in both domains and in each of the six subsets of use and, therefore, they are viewed as the primary recipients of professional development. The term teacher, as used in the model, includes school principals and other school administrators who, by and large, either see themselves as teachers or were teachers at some point. The emphasis on professional development for teachers is consistent with the view that, in the future, the capacity of schools to exploit the real power of ICT in education lies in its widespread uptake and use as distinct from the somewhat privileged access and use of the past in segmented and at times "balkanised" school cultures.

8. TASK AND PURPOSES

Our substantive point is this. Even though school administrators may employ various kinds of ICT tools, indeed even a whole computerised school information system, for seemingly school administrative and management tasks, the point and purpose of such use is, or should be twofold:
- Finding ways administratively and managerially to support teachers and students and allowing them access and use of school ICT systems so as to participate in, and contribute to, school administration and management processes as appropriate; and
- Creating and maintaining conditions that improve teaching and facilitate learning. This includes the development of students and teachers as learners, and in so doing permit and encourage wider teacher and student control over, and use of, ICT than in the past.

The development of schools in the direction of wider ICT access and use will necessitate a shift in mind-set. The shift involves entertaining and embracing alternative and new notions about the nature of schools as organisations and their own capacity to employ ICT in ways that they might not have considered yet. Anecdotal evidence and some case study research (Nolan and Lambert 2001) suggest that the shift is actually happening in specific schools and in educational policy agencies. For instance, the Ministry of Education has developed policies that:

1. encourage routine teacher use of the Internet to access curriculum and teaching resources; and
2. they support the adoption by schools of computerised school information systems usable across internal school levels and by a wide range of school staff.

One way by which the Ministry of Education encourages schools is by requiring that they meet reporting requirements by submitting school information and data electronically and in digital form.

By and large, in New Zealand the developments identified under points (1) and (2) have occurred in isolation. These have been separated by compartmentalised school structures and by different conceptions of how ICT might best be employed, either as learning or as administrative tools and commonly not by the same persons. A curriculum development and research project of the late 1980s and early 1990s (Nolan and McKinnon, 1991 2000) demonstrated how the uses identified in points (1) and (2) could be made interdependent. As students came to use the computer as learning tools, simultaneously the researchers and practitioners in the Project used various programs (e.g., spreadsheet and database programs) to administer the project, plan curriculum programmes, analyse trends in student achievement, and manage project budgets. This diversity of uses in the project was a forerunner to the now emerging contemporary concept of practitioners becoming competent ICT using professionals in a more integrated sense than the specialist ICT user of the past, e.g. the deputy principal managing the school timetable but not using ICT more extensively than this.

9.   LEVELS OF USE

Individuals who might be classified as 'all-round' competent ICT using professionals would fit within sub-set 4 of the model shown in figure 14.1, capable of employing a full range of ICT tools and processes within and across the L&T and A&M domains in any given school. Both ICT tools and processes are further distinguished in the model by the horizontal axis and in terms of the automating and informating levels of use identified by Fulmer (1995):

Automating is the routine processing by computer of school data associated with such administrative functions as the entry of student data into teacher maintained records, the processing of school accounts and the compilation of information for external agencies, e.g., the Ministry of Education

Informating is the generation, analysis and integration of information and data by computer to support school management and decision-making at various levels, viz the principal-senior management, departments and classrooms.

According to Fulmer (1995) automating occurs prior to informating processes and automating functions are of a lower order logically, conceptually and technically as indicated in the model by their placement below the horizontal axis line. Informating functions require ICT capabilities that are relatively more powerful and sophisticated even if (and preferably) relatively straightforward and simple to use although greater effort and understanding may be required to master them.

SUBSET 1: Teachers getting orientated to using ICT, developing awareness, gaining mastery of basic program functions and uses and experimenting with simple tasks in either or both the L&T and A&M domains, e.g. printing class lists or producing word processed signs for the classroom wall and using the Internet for email.

SUBSETS 2A AND 2B: Teachers having mastered the basic functions of one or more programs and using the programs for specific, probably loosely connected purposes, in a stand-alone fashion. For example in 2a, a teacher might be instructing students in the skills of word processing or showing them how to use an instructional program. In 2b, the same teacher might complete student reports on screen, fill-in student achievement forms and construct a class timetable.

SUBSETS 3A AND 3B: Teachers confidently and competently use a range of single purpose programs (e.g. a statistical package, CAD program) and integrated suites of programs within and across subject areas. For example in 3a, a teacher might assist students to design and execute an investigation and communicate findings using the following combination of tools, a digital camera, email and facsimile, spreadsheet, database, word processor, multimedia and web pages. In 3b, the same teacher might be using the same range of tools and purpose designed administrative tools to monitor and assess student achievement, do cohort analyses, and use the results of analyses to plan programmes linked to student achievement levels and interests.

SUBSET 4: Teachers using a range of ICT (as in 3a and 3b) as well as accessing and using the computerised school information system (e.g., the Pupil Files data base) to collaboratively examine and reflect upon the implications of achievement across class levels for school performance and improvement, and the formation of school policy, e.g., using the results of ANOVAs on student attendance and achievement in allocating students to classes.

10.   ZONES OF TRANSITION

In the model, the areas of intersection between circles are called *zones of transition.* The zones signify movement between levels of use and teacher expressions of interest to learn and do more. The movement and expressions of interest commonly occur when teachers: (i) have, or are developing, an awareness of the potential of the technology to support them to do their work better and more efficiently; and when (ii) they acknowledge the need to develop confidence and competency with a wider range of ICT tools and processes more powerful and versatile than those to which they are accustomed. The latter, in practice, often involves helping teachers make better use of tools they currently use, but which would remain under-utilised otherwise.

Temporally and spatially, zones of transition are places when and where it is timely and strategic to provide professional development and support which addresses three conditions that professional developers must identify and meet in order to achieve meaningful outcomes. They are:

– Accurate diagnosis of readiness and capacity for change in terms of existing ICT knowledge and use patterns and their location within one of the four levels of the model;

– Identification of concerns which may range from orientation to and awareness of ICT capabilities and tools that might next be mastered to worries about refinement of existing skills for implementation and use of systems and tools and the possibility of unintended consequences; and

– Regular and timely challenge, encouragement and support, in context, thereby demonstrating the relevance of the proposed new learning and its potential to produce outcomes of practical and real value.

11.   LEVELS OF USE AND LEVELS OF CONCERN

Experience of working with beginning ICT users, over many years, suggests that the case for overt, structured and carefully facilitated professional development (Nolan et al. 2001), in context, is most important at Level 1 of the model. The key is to first address and resolve the concerns of the persons seeking professional development and/or expected to take up and use a specific ICT tool. To this end, research reported elsewhere (Nolan and McKinnon 1989; Nolan et al. 1996) suggests the efficacy and effectiveness of the Concerns Based Adoption model (CBAM), and its two professional development instruments, *Level of Use* (LoU) and *Levels of Concern* (LoC), is most suitable for this purpose. Research using this model has been undertaken in schools, based on its use in development and research projects for implementing computerised school information systems to support school administration and management (see McKinnon and Nolan 1989; and Nolan et al. 1996, 2001 for more detailed explanations).

12. DISCUSSION

The refinement proposed here is that if the long-term goal to develop teachers as capable ICT-using professionals is to be realised, then professional development should be encouraged and facilitated on both the L&T and A&M pathways simultaneously, and in an integrative fashion. While this integrative aspect is not explicitly articulated and represented in the model of this paper, at this point, the key is likely to lie in the use of common tools and processes (e.g. a word processor and spreadsheet) for dual L&T and A&M purposes. In this way, variation of use at introduction is likely to consolidate skill acquisition and understanding of use and by reinforcing in the minds of users the multifunctional nature of the technology and the multiple tasks that it can usefully serve under their control.

With professional development viewed this way, teachers are more likely to shift the locus of control over the technology to themselves and become inured to using it routinely and to integrating it more effectively into their professional work and into the learning and teaching environments in which they work daily.

Beyond Level 1, the processes of CBAM remain useful; indeed, they provide essential tools for identifying professional development needs and for the structuring of ongoing professional development at higher levels of use. In so far as teachers have internalised locus of control at Level 1, then it is expected that they will take responsibility increasingly for initiating and conducting their own professional development through subsequent stages. Perhaps they will work collaboratively with peers and thereby promote and develop environments conducive to ongoing professional development and learning, thus promoting the growth of a school culture of the kind described at the outset that values both ICT and its use by competent ICT using professionals.

Importantly, while the locus of control over use of the professional development instruments of CBAM may shift, say, from external consultants to the teachers themselves, in order to continue being effectively used, the internal structure of the *Levels of Use* and *Levels of Concern* instruments should not be altered, at least not without good grounds for doing so based in experience. This is because empirical evidence of using them in many different professional development contexts has demonstrated the efficacy of the levels structure within each instrument. For example, with the Levels of Use instrument, mechanical use precedes routine use almost universally across different professional development contexts and integration, refinement and renewal follow in sequence, although the period for each may vary as a function of users' knowledge of, and competency in using, a particular ICT tool or system. For instance, a teacher already well versed in multimedia for both L&T and A&M purposes might move more quickly to working in a web-site development environment than a teacher wanting to do so but from only Level 1 or 2 competency with word processing. In this case, it may be necessary to acquire prerequisite knowledge and skills at an intermediate level and the *Levels of Use* and *Levels of Concern* instruments once operationalised for use at these levels would provide the specific professional development tools required.

Work done to date in this direction suggests the potential fruitfulness of using the CBAM instruments in this way, although ongoing research and development of a practical nature is required to specify the particular content of the *Levels of Use* and *Levels of Concern* instruments within each use level of the ICT Schematic Model of this paper.

13.   CONCLUSION

The model and associated ideas presented here are but another step on the pathway towards a developed, fully ramified and empirically validated explanation of the role and structure of professional development to foster teachers' mastery and use of ICT systems and tools for multiple purposes in education and assist them to more fully exploit the power of modern ICT for education. In New Zealand, a program of professional development work arising from the ideas that lead to this paper is soon to commence and it will consolidate and build upon the work done to date. It is our hope that others may see value in the model and the ideas of the paper and in due course report the outcomes of ongoing work at subsequent WG 3.7 ITEM Conferences.

REFERENCES

Cuban, L. (1999). Why are most teachers infrequent and restrained users of computers? *Report from the Fifth Annual Public Education Conference*, Vancouver. Available at: <http://www.bctf.bc.ca/parents/PublicEdConf/report99/appendix1.html>

Education Review Office. (2000). *In-Service training for teachers in New Zealand schools.* No.1. Wellington.

Fulmer, C.L. (1995). Maximising the Potential of Information Technology for Management Strategies for Interfacing the Technical Core of Education. In *Information Technology in Educational Management,* Barta, B-Z., Telem, M. and Gev, Y. (eds.). Chapman Hall, London

ITAG (2000, March). *ICT in Schools 1999.* Available at: <http://www.med.govt.nz/pbt/infotech/ictschools1999/index.html>

Lai, K.W., Pratt, K., & Trewern, A. (2001). *Learning with Technology: Evaluation of the Otago Technology Project.* Dunedin: The Community of Otago Trust.

Knezeck, G., Christensen, R., Hancock, R., & Shoho, A. (2000). Toward a Structural Model of Technology Integration. *Proceedings of the Annual Hawaii Educational Research Association.*

Ministry of Education (1999). *Interactive strategies for schools.* Ministry of Education, Wellington.

McKinnon, D.H. and Nolan, C.J.P. (2000) A longitudinal Study of Students' Attitudes towards Computers: Resolving an Attitude Decay Paradox. *Journal of Research on Computing in Education* 32(3), 325-335.

McKinnon, D.H. & Nolan, C.J.P. (1989). Using Computers in Education: A Concerns-based Approach to Professional Development for Teachers. *The Australian Journal of Educational Technology,* 5(2) 113-131.

Nolan, C.J.P., Brown, M.A. & Graves, B. (2001). MUSAC in New Zealand: From Grass Roots to System-wide in a Decade. In. *Information Technology in Educational Management: Synthesis of experience, research and future perspectives on computer-assisted school information systems* Visscher. A.J., Wild P. and Fung, A.C.W (eds). Kluwer, Holland.

Nolan, C.J.P. and Lambert, M. (2001). Information Systems for Leading and Managing Schools: Changing the Paradigm. In *Pathways to Institutional Improvement: Information Technology in Educational Management,* Nolan, C.J.P., Fung, A.C.W and Brown, M.A. (Eds.). Kluwer, Holland.

Nolan, C.J.P. and McKinnon, D.H. (2000) Integrative Secondary School Education and IT Augmented Learning. *7th SEAMEO INNOTECH International Conference: Knowledge Networking in the World of Learning.* Manila: Philippines.

Nolan, C.J.P., & Ayres, D.A. (1996). Developing a Good Information System for Schools: The New Zealand Experience. *International Journal of Educational Research*, 25(4), 307-321.

Nolan, C.J.P., Ayres, D.A. Dunn, S. and McKinnon, D.H. (1996) Implementing Computerised School Information Systems: Case Studies from New Zealand. *International Journal of Educational Research*, 25(5), 335-349.

Nolan, C.J.P. (1995) The Development of Computer-assisted School Administration in New Zealand. In *Information Technology and Educational Management,* Barta, B.Z., Telem, M. and Gev. Y. (eds.). Chapman and Hall, London.

Nolan, C.J. P., McKinnon, D.H. and Soler, J. (1992) Computers in Education: Achieving equitable Access and Use, *Journal of Research on Computing in Education,* 24(3), 299-314.

Nolan, C.J.P. and McKinnon, D.H. (1991) A Case Study of Curriculum Innovation in New Zealand: The Freyberg Integrated Studies Project, *Curriculum Perspectives,* 11: 4, 1-10.

Stewart, D. J., 2000. *Tomorrow's Principal Today.* Kanuka Grove Press, Palmerston North New Zealand.

Visscher, A.J. (1996). Information Technology in Educational Management as an Emerging Discipline. *International Journal of Educational Research,* 25(4), 291-296.

SECTION 5

REPORTS FROM DISCUSSION GROUPS

15

THE MANAGEMENT OF E-LEARNING

Alex Fung and Jenilyn Ledesma
With Abdelmalek Benzekri, Margaret Clarke, Celso Perdomo-Gonzalez, Jorge Rodriguez-Diaz, and Harald Yndestad

Key words: E-learning, technology, teaching and learning

PREAMBLE

The discussion group explored and addressed several areas regarding the management of e-learning. Building on the discussion, six issues were identified at the end of the conference. These six issues have provided the structure for this discussion paper. Each issue is discussed separately.

1.   DEFINITIONS OF E-LEARNING

The world of education has now moved into an era of e-learning, and the existence of technology has reached a point where it challenges the traditional education system. Keywords are highlighted in an attempt to define and discuss e-learning and its associated issues. These keywords include:
– Use of Internet / Intranet / Extranet
– Synchronous / Asynchronous
– Integration of Media Technology.
    The following were some of the definitions of e-learning.

"e" means electronic media to help enhance student education. It also means computer-mediated (based) learning, and can be both off campus (remote) as well as on campus (present). It is also about time and space.

e-learning is a technologically driven education. It means computer-assisted learning, with additional support from teachers, guides and utilizing learning objects.

From education to e-learning, the learning activities and roles change. In this digital era, there are new database technologies, new structures, new delivery modes, and new system concepts. Even the roles of teachers and students change. Teachers do not just teach; they coach, instruct and advise. Students do not just listen; they learn how to learn and how to be creative and proactive.

2.   VISIONS OF E-LEARNING [DREAMS FOR THE NEW EDUCATION SYSTEM]

So, what change will occur after the introduction of e-learning? Some visions and dreams for the new education system are presented.

Dream 1:   The Professor or 'teacher' comes to the class not to deliver knowledge, but to listen, discuss and share information and experiences with the students.

Dream 2:   Education could either be group collaboration or individualized learning, or both. Learning becomes multidimensional, more customized and personalized, catering for the individual needs of learners and differences between learners.

Dream 3:   To have equity or 'education for all learners'. Life-long and life-wide learning is about breadth and depth not restricted to the academic realm.

Dream 4:   The final goal of e-learning – the creation, interaction and generation of knowledge, skills and competencies in learners.

3.   HOW TO GET THERE WITH THE SUPPORT OF TECHNOLOGY

Utilizing technology has the potential to realize these dreams (new ways of learning). Change management is needed, including the management of change within the organization, changes to the roles of individuals, taking account of globalisation and social as well as structural changes. Integration and adaptation of technology into other sub-systems and parameters of education are also required (see Figure 15-1). Learning issues, either by self or by groups, need to be identified to better enhance e-learning.

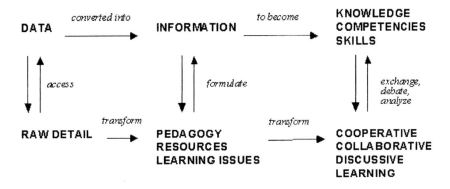

Figure 15.1. Integration and adaptation of technology into other sub-systems and parameters of education

Technology as an end it itself: is what we can refer to as learning technology: about systems of communication, parts of a computer, learning to use a text editor, navigating the Internet and so on.

Technology as a tool: corresponds to the conception most in use: doing practical things, allowing the technical operation of machines and the running of software.

Technology as a teaching resource: it can be used to look at subjects as diverse as mathematics and social studies, and also to reinforce as well as widen our knowledge of them.

4. CHANGES NEEDED TO SUPPORT E-LEARNING

Several changes are seen as necessary to support e-learning. Firstly, there is a need for standardization to assure inter- and intra-comparability. Education can take advantage of e-learning by preparing digitised materials/activities to be accessible on the Internet, which can be appropriately used as learning objects for the learners. Universities, schools and other institutions can become places for delivery, communication and interaction. There should be ongoing, dynamic evaluation by feedback. Freeware should be encouraged instead of commercial IT software packages, for equity to students accessing information anywhere anytime. Cultural and mindset changes are also needed, as well as the re-organization of technology for better delivery of learning. Customisation from a 'train system' (mass production) to a 'taxi system' (flexible) is required, although infrastructure and traffic should be considered. Teachers' roles should be more versatile and inventive. The role of educational institutions may be perceived to be as one that maintains and develop culture (cultural preservation and knowledge creation), but at the same time to contribute to the development of other areas (professional skills development, societal needs). Different sets of skills, dispositions and competences are necessary to help students respond to new content, new ideas and settings. In short, education and e-learning should be integral to education.

5.   DIFFERENT ROLES TO MAKE E-LEARNING OPERATIONAL

To make e-learning operational, different availabilities and roles are presently required. People with passion to promote or "champion" the vision (dream) are needed.
– Teaching and learning: Collaborative learning vs. collaborative (team) teaching
– Roles: movers, shakers, visionaries, enforcers, advocators (preachers), educators, diffusers, developers, makers, creators, planners, actors
The potential threat of multi-national corporations dominating education should encourage educational institutions to cooperate, network and organize at different levels (public, private, schools, universities).
– School and university: the shift from the trains (too static and compartmentalized) to the taxi (flexible) system in education delivery is needed for a smooth and coherent progression from school and university to the workplace, and eventually for life long learning.
  With the new actors / roles,
– Students change from passive receiver to protagonist of the process;
– Teachers possess important organizational skills, and stop being the source of information to become learning facilitators.
The presence of new demands in society will also continue the formation of new actors and roles, all of which will be actively participating in the promotion process, with the capacity and ability to modify the methodology applied to the teaching and learning paradigm from beginning to end.

6.   OTHER ISSUES AND POINTS TO PONDER

New ways of thinking, although problematic, lead to new pedagogy. There is no doubt that the use of technology can better support this change. Not only do teachers and learners need to be adaptable but they also need to be more proactive. This adds value to the use of ICT in education. Hence, there is a need to re-invent and re-engineer the education system. But, how can one turn this process into something operational? What kind of organizations can give this endorsement?

IFIP is one organization that can help ensure that e-learning is given the consideration it merits e.g. in giving endorsements to these ideas, top down and/or bottom up action plans. Strategic channels are needed to raise the concern of different actors at different levels of this important aspect of education.

16

MANAGEMENT SYSTEMS IN THE CLASSROOM
Prospects for theFuture

Leonard Newton and Adrie Visscher
With Marko Bajec, Alison Kennedy, Coach Kereteletswe, Maureen Lambert, Pat Nolan, Arthur Tatnall and Chris Thorn

Key words: Management Information Systems, Knowledge Management Systems, classrooms, teachers

1. INTRODUCTION

Improving education is a prominent theme in many countries and, in the drive to raise standards, increasing quantities of data about pupils' attainment and progress is being generated. These data, collected at many levels in the educational system, provide a means to both monitor the performance of individual schools and to 'benchmark' and set targets at local and national levels.

Management Information Systems (MIS) enable the collation and interrogation of data at whole school, class and individual student levels. Such data, when collected from standardised national tests, permit comparisons to be made between similar schools against benchmark performance levels. However, this process may sometimes be contentious and raises questions about the validity of the chosen performance indicators and the instruments used to assess them. At another level of organisation, the impact of performance data on teachers' actions in the classroom remains problematic with fears that a teacher's focus may be too heavily directed to the measures of performance at the possible expense of teaching quality.

This paper examines some issues related to the use of MIS in classroom contexts and considers some possible future needs of teachers that may present challenges to the designers of the next generation of MIS tools.

2.   CURRENT USES OF MIS - SOME PROBLEMS

The Management Information Systems available in many schools and colleges offer a wide range of administrative functions, and generally perform these functions very well. Despite this, however, in most school systems not much use seems to be made of the information provided by MIS to directly affect what goes on in the classroom. In higher education, the evidence suggests that in many universities, partly because of the way that data are stored and accessed, absolutely no use can be made of data to improve teaching and learning. The data contained in typical MIS is intended to be used *only* for administrative purposes. The reason for this is related to the perceived stakeholders that the system was designed to serve. In most schools and universities, no consideration appears to have been given to the teaching function in MIS design. Thus, a tension exists between the different purposes of MIS in education: systems designed to provide school management information (for example, budget control, attendance figures, aggregated student performance data) are unlikely to adequately serve the information needs of teachers for classroom teaching purposes.

Schools, both individually and within systems, already possess robust management information systems, but evidence and anecdote indicate that teachers and managers under use them. This under-use raises questions about the competences required for decision-making using MIS and the capacity of users to implement them in their day-to-day activity. Requirement analyses of MIS for use in higher education suggest that it may not be possible to meet the diverse range of requirements for MIS in a single piece of software. In both school and higher education contexts, opportunities are missed to make use of information (much of it already stored in the MIS) to improve the quality of teaching and learning. Thus, a key issue to be addressed and resolved is how MIS users might more effectively exploit their potential in individual classrooms: particularly in ways that support both the broad standards agenda and, more importantly, the achievements of individual learners.

3.   CHALLENGES FOR THE FUTURE

In order to frame the subsequent discussion, we address the following groups of questions:

1. Given what is being done already, in which new and desirable ways can IT systems further be developed to support teaching and learning practices?
2. What are the benefits hoped for in new MISs? How and why might these be achieved?
3. How can we promote the use of these systems and how might the conditions of teachers be changed to facilitate the use of MIS? What are the design and implementation strategies required?

To address the first of these themes, we need to consider the weaknesses detected in the current state of MIS development, and in the use of MIS. Many of the weaknesses arise from the loose coupling of the design features of MIS to the needs of classroom teachers. Therefore, it is necessary to disassociate 'oversight systems' for accountability (which is about the management functions of an educational system, and instructional support systems) and system use that supports teaching and learning. Asking a single system to deliver both accountability and diagnosis (at least, at the individual level) provides mixed incentives for end users and significant design problems for designers. It is vital to remember that teaching and learning is a social process and that information that is relevant for making long-term decisions about staffing, changes in curriculum and standards, etc. is not appropriate for making day-to-day decisions.

Progress is required in at least two different areas. First, IT systems in education should be designed with the target populations in mind. This would be an improvement on the present situation where an unending series of add-on modules form a loose amalgam of disjoint sub-systems that fail to adequately meet the needs of any constituency of users. Second, 'knowledge repositories' for teachers are required as distinct from systems designed for managers. Such knowledge repositories might better support teachers as they search for resources to address the learning needs of their students, and their own personal and professional learning needs. A key task is, therefore, to identify the kinds of data and information that would be of use to classroom teachers.

With respect to the second question-set: namely, the benefits hoped for in new MIS, and how these might be realised; the needs of users should be more fully considered. To this end, the benefits of a MIS are best identified through examination of the requirements of different constituencies and linking these to system characteristics. Strategic decision-making can be better supported if the relevant outcome variables are tracked. For example, many school districts target particular areas of professional development. An appropriate evaluative framework for monitoring professional development might do the following: capture levels of staff participation; identify staff members' perception of the quality of the training; and measures of the impact of training. Taken together these elements would provide a coherent framework for judging the efficacy of a specific resource allocation strategy.

In the case of a learning support system, better alignment between pedagogy; learning standards; standards-based curriculum; and standards-aligned assessment could allow MIS designers to develop coherent support frameworks. For example, these frameworks might categorise curricular resources, professional development opportunities, and alternative assessment strategies. A framework could match student strengths and weaknesses with appropriate educational materials. Future MIS may therefore provide teachers with decision support systems that could enable them to make better judgements about the selection of particular curriculum resources for particular purposes. Such systems would require data entries to be clearly linked to specific curricular goals or standards. This capability would allow teachers to focus more time on teaching and less time on locating appropriate resources.

Student achievement in education is characterised by more than grade scores. Life-long learning records and portfolios provide a rich evidence base of the diverse achievements of learners and will contain more information than attainment records against benchmarked tests. Evidence of students' skills and achievements in other areas of their experience needs to be recorded and this evidence may or may not need to be digitised for storage in a MIS. However, the use of electronically stored portfolios raises questions of data protection and ownership of material; it may require a significant shift in perspective on issues of accountability and on the mutual understanding of the teacher-student dynamic. In any event, good portfolio development involves filtering and selection of information against clearly articulated standards and, in this respect, MIS could bring coherence to the portfolio process. Groupware systems could also be useful in this regard, as they offer an environment for group discussions. Using such systems students can open discussions on problems they would like to solve, and teachers can participate and help students to solve the problem. This is especially useful for students who have difficulties in being active in the classroom. Such developments are not currently addressed well in existing MIS and should feature more centrally in future developments.

The use of Knowledge Management Systems (KMS) as delivery systems for educational content may incorporate 'tracking' utilities that enable information on student progress through the KMS to be recorded in ways similar to those currently found in Integrated Learning Systems such as *'Successmaker'*.

Portal technology holds the prospect of bringing MIS closer to end-users, as it endeavours to facilitate access and use. Development in portal technology is essentially user-centric: this means that designers are expected to spend much more time on acquiring specific requirements from different system users. Potentially, this might offer teachers and managers new opportunities to define what they really want.

Other possible classroom uses of MIS could include early diagnosis of problems likely to be encountered by a particular student by examination of achievement data for that student from previous years. Use of comparative data from a MIS, including demographic data, to provide examples for use in teaching and student assignments may be valuable too.

The third set of questions concern the design and implementation strategies required to facilitate wider use of MIS by teachers. A major issue arising from the earlier discussion is the need for MIS to offer a good match between the requirements of users. Thus, it might be asked: how can a MIS be built that is adaptable for use by the incumbents of different roles, i.e. that a system that is responsive to different kinds of 'role-use'. In this way the MIS of the future might more adequately reflect the needs and demands of teachers and managers.

In the case of management systems, their widespread use would require a shift from a focus on mere accountability to a more holistic view of assessment and its facilitation as part of a larger evaluation model. A more effective way to do this work is to find a district that has most of the basic technical and social elements in place and to co-opt its support in the process of system design, development and implementation. The design focus would need to be on the information needs of teachers - not just on the reporting needs of the larger educational system. Traditional approaches to MIS design show little likelihood of penetrating the realities of classroom practice and thus supporting and enhancing it. A design project that examined both the ways in which teachers create and use diagnostic information on the one hand, and then locate and integrate appropriate curricular resources would be an exciting and compelling departure from traditional approaches. It might, indeed, suggest directions for the future that are potentially more beneficial for a much wider constituency of educational professionals and be more responsive to their interests and concerns.

4.   CONCLUDING REMARKS

It is clear that educational users have different needs and purposes for MIS depending on their organisational context and role. The kinds of information required at different levels within education (individual / class / department / school etc) vary and may be available within a single MIS, but not all users need access to all information. In the future, some features of portal technology might have relevance in helping users find value in the information made available to them by MIS. Currently available MIS have limitations. Both users and designers need to appreciate that information made available to users through MIS requires interpretation to inform decisions and action. At the level of the classroom, MIS capabilities should be developed explicitly to address the needs of teachers. It is therefore legitimate to ask what the features might be of support systems for teachers mediated by MIS. A key question must be to ask what value a MIS adds to educational endeavours in classrooms. If we keep asking these questions, we may be successful in developing MIS that will help us to improve the quality of instruction as well as the performance of students and schools!

17

CORE COMPETENCES FOR ITEM
A Model

Ian Selwood and Christopher O'Mahony
with Rakesh Bhatt, Bill Davy, Margaret Haughey, Hatano Kazuhiko, Javier Osorio, and Tuulikki Paturi.

Key words: Competences, training, management, decision-making

1.   INTRODUCTION

As part of the 2002 ITEM Conference, a Discussion Group was formed with the mandate to explore the core competences required for ITEM. It was recognised by the group that, whereas IT for Educational Management has existed in educational institutions for almost 20 years, the history of its introduction was characterised by a generally ad-hoc approach to implementation. In particular, it was perceived that attempts to introduce new technologies into educational institutions often lacked coherent and effective training programmes, to the extent that the literature reports unsatisfactory use of ICT in teaching, learning and administration (Lambert & Nolan 2002, Ofsted 2002, Newton 2002).

The discussion group sought to develop a model or framework, which would enable educational institutions to plan their ITEM training and achieve an ITEM-competent staff.

2.   BACKGROUND

In discussing the issue of how to train school managers to use managerial school information systems Visscher and Branderhost (2001) point out that there is strong empirical evidence that user training strongly influences the degree of information system usage. Selwood (1995) highlighted the problems concerning the lack of differentiation of training for different levels of school personnel in the England and Wales – Headteachers, trained alongside school secretaries. More recently, Selwood and Drenoyianni (1997) discussed the problems of training senior managers in the use of their school's Management Information System (MIS) to support their decision-making. Donnelly (2000) claimed that there were three levels of training appropriate to both the leadership team and administrative staff – training in generic software, training in the use of school-specific MIS software, and training in the use of the Internet. Additionally he stressed the need for the leadership team to be trained in how to use data to improve educational standards. Visscher and Branderhost (2001) specified five skill areas that they felt were needed by school staff:

1. Recognition of the value of information systems, and development of a school policy;
2. Determination of the type of information they need for their work, or for a specific problem;
3. Discovering how they can get information from their school MIS;
4. Interpreting information from their school MIS;
5. Using information from their school MIS for decision-making and policy-evaluation.

In the USA the Collaborative for Technology Standards for School Administrators have produced a set of "Technology Standards for School Administrators" (TSSA Collaborative 2001). However, whilst these are comprehensive they cover all aspects of technology including its use to support teaching and learning. These standards and are aimed at not only school based education managers, but also those at a district level. Thus, they need deconstructing in order to extract standards for ITEM.

In England and Wales, currently the government is in the process of promoting its Information Management Strategy (IMS 2000). As part of this, two documents concerned with competences have been produced: one is a self-evaluation form for Information Management and ICT Competences (DfES, 2002a); the other is aimed at identifying who does what in terms of administration activities (DfES 2002b).

The group felt that whilst many of the documents referred to above were useful, in highlighting the problems and some of the competences that were needed for the effective use of ITEM, none of them really described the core competences for ITEM. Furthermore, those that did detail competences tended to concentrate on operational competences at the expense of tactical and strategic competences.

3. THE MODEL

3.1 The X Axis: ITEM Dimensions

We believe that the best way to open the lid on the ITEM black-box is to deconstruct our basic terms. Thus, four core dimensions present themselves – Information, Technology, Education and Management. ITEM links these four dimensions inextricably. It is in the interactions of these four dimensions that ITEM has its uniqueness.

3.2 The Y Axis: Organisational Levels – Operational, Tactical, and Strategic

The management process is primarily concerned with decision-making. Drawn from the management literature decision making can occur at three different levels operational, tactical, and strategic. Whenever for example, headteachers and governing bodies in a school form a vision of where the school is going establish aims and objectives prioritise them and develop a plan for the accomplishment of these objectives, they are involved in strategic decision-making. Whenever they are making decisions concerned with the implementation of the school's development plan (e.g. appoint or dismiss teaching or other staff), their decisions may be considered as tactical. Finally, whenever they have to carry out clear and specific tasks (e.g. ordering supplies) they are making operational decisions. An alternative approach in considering these organisational levels is to do so in terms of the degree of structured thinking, whereby operational decisions are highly structured, tactical decisions are semi-structured, and strategic decisions tend to be highly unstructured.

3.3 The Z Axis – Stages of Growth

The members of the discussion group felt that it was important to reflect the degree of sophistication of the organisation's IT effort. To this end, the group looked to well-exercised 'stages of growth' theories, the most popular in this arena being Nolan (1979), Visscher (1991) and Galliers & Sutherland (1991).

Each of these theorists offered a model with certain relevance to the ITEM competence debate. Both the Nolan and Galliers & Sutherland models were perceived as too generic for the ITEM domain. At the same time, although the Visscher model was perceived as being the most relevant, we wanted to modify the stage labels to more closely reflect stages of sophistication. After some debate, the stage labels chosen were therefore Initiation, Expansion, and Embedded.

Table 17-1. Stages of growth compared [Please provide a caption for this table]

Stage	Nolan	Visscher	Galliers & Sutherland
I	Initiation	Initiation	Ad Hocracy
II	Contagion		Starting the Foundations
III	Control	Expansion	Centralised Dictatorship
IV	Integration	Integration	Democratic Dialectic and Cooperation.
V	Data Administration		Entrepreneurial Opportunity
VI	Maturity		The Age of Aquarius

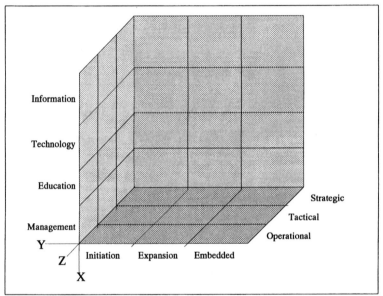

Figure 17-1. The proposed three dimensional model of ITEM Competences

3.4   Advantages of the ITEM Competence Model

The proposed model offered certain advantages, as follows:
- It enables us to map existing policies and programmes, and to investigate goodness of fit of those policies and programmes;
- It enables us to map ITEM competences to existing job descriptions within educational institutions;
- It is platform-independent;
- It is descriptive;
- It is prescriptive;

- It helps us in the development of more appropriate policies and programmes for ITEM competences.
- It assists in the development of an appropriate post-graduate ITEM curriculum;
- It enables the certification of other courses against the criteria noted in these competences.

3.5 The Dimension Space

	Operational	Tactical	Strategic
Information	Data	Information	Knowledge
Technology	Transaction Processing	Management Information Systems	Knowledge Management / EIS / Expert Systems
Education	Routine	Projects	Visioning
Management	Individual	Team / Department	Whole-School

3.6 Operational Competences

	Initiation	Expansion	Embedded
Information	Recognise & edit data	Link & Interpret data	Leverage & Exploit data
Technology	Initiate & Manipulate transactions	Link & Interpret transactions	Leverage & Exploit transactions
Education	Routine Recording	Routine Reporting	Exception Reporting
Management	Organise my tasks	Prioritise my tasks	Control & Transform my tasks

3.7 Tactical Competences

	Initiation	Expansion	Embedded
Information	Recognise & edit information	Link & Interpret Information	Leverage & Exploit Information
Technology	Initiate & Manipulate MIS	Link & analyse MIS	Leverage & Exploit MIS
Education	Recognise projects	Link & interpret Projects	Leverage & Exploit projects
Management	Organise my team	Control & Prioritise my team	Leverage & Transform my team.

3.8   Strategic Competences

	Initiation	Expansion	Embedded
Information	Recognise & manipulate knowledge	Link & interpret knowledge	Leverage & exploit knowledge
Technology	Initiate & Manipulate EIS	Link & analyse EIS	Leverage & Exploit EIS
Education	Recognise Vision	Communicate Vision	Leverage & Exploit (share) Vision
Management	Organise my institution	Control & Prioritise my institution	Leverage & Transform my institution

4.   CONCLUSIONS AND RECOMMENDATIONS

The Discussion Group had thus identified 36 core ITEM competences – four dimensions (Information, Technology, Education, Management) at three levels (Operational, Tactical, Strategic) for three degrees of sophistication (Initiation, Expansion, Embedded). It is apparent that as one gains competence at one level and moves to the next, the cognitive processes and decision-making involved move from Structured (Level 1) to Semi-structured (Level 2) to Unstructured (Level 3). As a corollary to this, it will be expected that Level 1 competence is a pre-requisite for transition to Level 2, and Level 2 competence is a pre-requisite for transition to Level 3.

The Group recommended that subsequent work should be devoted to two key activities:

a) To populate each of the 36 core ITEM competences with practical, real-life examples; and

b) To use this ITEM Competence Grid to benchmark existing ITEM curricula;

As time passes, the technology landscape will inevitably change, with different competences emerging. It will be important to review the framework after two years.

REFERENCES

DfEE (2000). *Information Management Strategy for Schools and LEAS.*
   http://www.dfee.gov.uk/ims/summary.brief.shtm. DfEE. London
DfES (2002a). *Staff ICT competences framework 21 Aug.*
   http://www.teachernet.gov.uk/docbank/index.cfm?id=2820. DfES. London
DfES (2002b).*Who does what Aug 21.*
   http://www.teachernet.gov.uk/docbank/index.cfm?id=2821. DfES. London

Donnelly, J. (2000). Information Management Strategy for Schools and Local Education Authorities – Report on Training Needs. http://dfes.gov.uk/ims/JDReportfinal.rtf . DfES, London

Galliers, R.G. & Sutherland A.R., (1991), Information systems management and strategy formulation: the 'stages of growth' model revisited, *Journal of Information Systems*, 1, 1991.

Lambert, M.J., & Nolan, C.J.P., (2003). Managing learning environments in schools: developing ICT capable teachers. In Management of Education in The Information Age - The Role of ICT. Edited by Selwood I, Fung A, O'Mahony C. Kluwer for IFIP. London

Newton, L., (2003). Management and the use of ICT in subject teaching – integration for learning. In Management of Education in The Information Age - The Role of ICT. Edited by Selwood I, Fung A, O'Mahony C. Kluwer for IFIP. London

Nolan, R.L., (1979), Managing the Crises in Data Processing, *Harvard Business Review*, 57, 2, March 1979, pp 115-126.

Ofsted (2002). *ICT in Schools, Effect of Government Initiatives.* http://www.ofsted.gov.uk/public/docs01/ictreport.pdf . DfES , London.

Selwood, I. (1995). The Development of ITEM in England and Wales in *Information Technology in Educational Management*. Edited by Ben Zion Barta, Moshe Telem and Yaffa Gev. Chapman Hall for IFIP, London, UK.

Selwood, I.D. & Drenoyianni, H. (1997). Administration, Management and IT in Education in *Information Technology in Educational Management for the Schools of the Future.* Edited by Fung A, Visscher A, Barta B and Teather D. Chapman & Hall for IFIP. London, UK.

TSSA (2001). *Technology Standards for Scool Administrators.* http://cnets.iste.org/tssa/docs/tssa.pdf . TSSA Collaborative/ISTE, Eugene.

Visscher, A.J. & Brandhorst, E.M. (2001). How should School Managers be Trained for Managerial School Information System Usage? In *Pathways to Institutional Improvement with Information Technology in Educational Management.* Edited by Nolan, C.J.P., Fung, A.C.W., & Brown, M.A. Kluwer for IFIP. London

Visscher, A.J., (1991), School administrative computing: a framework for analysis, *Journal of Research on Computing in Education*, 24, 1, Fall 1991, pp 1-19.

Index of contributors

Key word index